D1359732

*19 Tips and Techniques for your Success!*

# BEACONS
## *of*
# LIGHT
## *on*
# LEADERSHIP

## DR. MAC MCGUIRE

McGuire
& Associates Consulting

# DEDICATION

Let me dedicate this book to my wonderful wife, best friend, and life companion, Lin. She has been instrumental in making this book a reality. Her calm demeanor and commitment to me cannot be overstated. She is the light of my life and is a stabilizing influence in times of concern. I would also like to take this opportunity to thank the many people who helped me along the way, my friends, my mentors, and those who always did the wrong thing regarding Leadership so I could learn how not to do things.

To Lin, My Best Friend

# FOREWORD

For many years now, a number of my students at the University of Texas Professional Development Center (where I have taught for over 23 years) have asked me to put leadership information into a book. This information comes from my life of over 30 years in the United States Army both as a civil service employee as well as while on active duty with the Texas Army National Guard. I have read in excess of 3,500 books about leadership and believe I can contribute some worthy information. Some of this information is the result of lessons learned from bad judgment and errors I have made – hopefully not that many times.

I have had many people help me while writing this book. One, Ernest Seitz, helped me edit this book. His attention to detail and honesty made it a better tome. Ernest is an American hero with his military service and his subsequent career in education as a principal, assistant superintendent, and educational consultant.

Lindsey Wrinkle, MBA, also did an edit from her standpoint which was very helpful. She is in the early stages of her career but her insight was important for obvious reasons.

Some students at Taylor Independent School District Media Class, under the wise tutelage of Ms. Dawn Fischer, also developed some ideas about the book cover.

Others who have helped me along this path of discovery are Charley Kelley, Kent Hemingson, Liz Coker, W. C. Inmon, Betty McCormick, COL (R) Danny Kohler, LTC (R) Bill Lee, SGM (R) Andy Delcuze, COL

(R) Bill Clark, Michelle O'Reilly, Vic Figurelli, and a great mentor in COL (R) David Biscomb.

Lin, my wife, also did a great deal of editing and spent long hours devoted to making the book make sense of some of my ramblings. She, as is mentioned in the dedication, has been instrumental in this book being brought to light. I am very grateful for her friendship, love, and devotion.

# TABLE OF CONTENTS

# PRELUDE

To begin this study or read, we need to outline what is to be covered in this book. I chose these particular tips and techniques (strategies) because I believe they are truly the essence of leadership. None of these are necessarily in order of importance except number 1 as I will discuss later in the book.

Each tip, technique, or strategy will be discussed at some length with major teaching points, designated "TP:" indicating key takeaways from the paragraph or point being made. It is my hope that the teaching points drive home the essence of what I am saying about what I have learned, read, and experienced.

## 19 TIPS AND TECHNIQUES (STRATEGIES) OF LEADERSHIP:

1. Trust.
2. Teambuilding.
3. Exhibit honesty and integrity.
4. Vision.
5. Be ethical.
6. Communicate constantly.
7. Develop others.
8. Insist on excellence and measures.
9. Praise.
10. Set the right example.
11. Empower your people.
12. Courage.

13. Confidence.
14. Be decisive, persistent, and patient.
15. Take intelligent calculated risks.
16. Sense of urgency.
17. Be loyal.
18. Listen.
19. Dedicated and available.

Leaders must be able to objectively evaluate themselves regarding their strengths, weaknesses, opportunities, and threats (SWOT). I recommend listing the top three items in each part of your SWOT such as the top three strengths, top three weaknesses, etc. The best way to accomplish that evaluation is with a group of mentors. Mentors should be wiser or more knowledgeable than you. I recommend surrounding yourself with people you believe to be smarter than you. Some of my mentors really helped me by modeling, discussing, and evaluating my personal and work life while assisting me with detailing my aspirations. My self-evaluations were a little shallow at first as I am sure yours will be as well. Mentors should always be allowed to tell you the truth about you. Sometimes my mentors were complimentary of my skills and sometimes they were critical of me. Mentors can really assist you IF you are willing to listen, make an assessment of the validity of their comments, and be willing to change your thoughts, skills, and knowledge.

---

**TP: Make sure you evaluate yourself honestly and preferably with trusted mentors. Don't ever believe you have all the answers . . . ever.**

---

As I mentioned above, the number 1 strategy for being a successful leader is to build relationships through a dedicated vision . . . in both your work life as well as your personal life. It will be difficult to build relationships if you do not know where you are going, both professionally and personally.

I once heard a famous quote about Leadership that has been burned into my memory. It has been attributed in different forms to a number of people, so I will paraphrase as, "People will not remember what you said, they will probably not remember what you did, they may not remember your name, but they will remember how you made them feel! Make them feel important."

Ms. Porter was my third grade teacher at Blossom Elementary School, Blossom, Texas, (east of Paris, Texas; good place to Google if you might not know where it is). She was very instrumental in my development as a person and as a student because of her positive attitude and encouraging nature. She was very professional, even as an elementary school teacher, and wore high heels and pearls almost every day. She would whisper encouraging words to me, and she touched my heart. I will never forget how she made me feel, ever. For a country boy who was incredibly shy, she made a difference!

---

**TP: Leaders must build relationships with others. Making others feel important and heard is critical to those relationships. Before your employees will care about you and your organizational needs, they need to know you care about them.**

---

It is my firm belief that the items listed above and in the subsequent pages of this book will enable you to become a better leader in the future. Becoming a better leader is not easy. It is very difficult because you must keep growing to achieve true "Big L" Leadership status and retain it. "Big L" signifies an attempt to address all of the 19 tips and techniques (strategies) in a positive manner.

I designed this book to be read from front to back or to focus in on a specific strategy. I recommend that you read it from front to back to understand the integration of the strategies with each other and how they are all a part of Leadership. Leadership "Big L" is the collection of a number of skill sets (19 is my number).

---

TP: In order to become a true Leader (Big L), you need to cognitively understand the connectivity of all of the 19 strategies. They are all linked to each other.

---

A defining study by the Hay Group (Lamb & McGee, 2004) had a number of conclusions germane to this book. The research found the following factors influenced employee satisfaction regarding Leadership:

1. trust and confidence in top leadership was the single highest predictor of employee satisfaction,

2. effective communication directed toward an understanding of the overall business strategy (strategic plan),

3. helping employees understand how they contribute to achieving key business objectives (paint a picture of success and put them in it),

4. the effective sharing of information concerning how the organization is doing, and,

5. outlining the employee contribution in relation to the business strategy (a strategic plan with defined objectives and accountability).

---

TP: Trust and confidence in your Leadership is paramount to employee satisfaction. Employee satisfaction is critical to organizational achievement under your watch (as a leader).

---

At the end of each chapter, I will take a moment and pose some questions I normally receive in teaching about Leadership. The questions below are thoughts for you personally or could be used with a group doing a book study of this book.

My intent for this book is to have a conversation with you about how to become a successful and effective Leader (Big L). Good luck to you on this Journey . . . Let's get started!

# LEADERSHIP DEFINED

First let me lay some groundwork by defining what Leadership means to me based upon my research, my experience, and my teaching events.

Leadership is about being very intentional and deliberate in your actions. If you constantly find yourself a fire-fighter at work, running from problem to problem without real priorities, this book may be of great value to you. A leader must be intentional and deliberate about the priorities at work. YOU owe your people a list of the top three priorities at work. What are they? How do you know? Are they changing based upon customers' needs? Are you staying ahead of the competition? If you are in a school system, are your students continually improving? If in a hospital environment, are the satisfaction scores for patients and families still trending upward?

---

TP: Make sure as the Leader you have <u>identified</u> and <u>communicated</u> the right priorities and there are not too many. Three is the best number of priorities!

---

I teach numerous classes on Leadership. Sometimes in one of the classes, a student or adult will ask, "What should I do if there are no priorities?" Every leader at any level including informal leaders, owe employees the priorities of work. Leaders must designate and emphasize the most important priorities of work for employees. A constant changing of priorities or "firefighting" (running from one priority to another) is counterproductive and minimizes organizational and individual effectiveness.

TP: After the Leader identifies and communicates the top three priorities, make sure all of your people understand them and are working on them. It is critical that Leaders ensure everyone, and I do mean everyone, knows the organizational priorities.

As you do roundings (moving about the office and talking to your people in the morning and afternoon; I suggest early morning and midafternoon), you need to ask the employees what they are working on. Their work must be connected to one of those three priorities you have identified for the office. If you have selected the priorities wisely, you will address around 80% of the most pressing requirements of your office. If what the employees are doing is not related to the work priorities you have established, you must redirect their efforts aligning the work with the top three priorities.

Leadership is also about accepting personal responsibility for those who work for you, your boss, and for the organizational priorities that have been established and communicated to all. If someone makes a mistake and they work for you, it is your mistake. Two of my previous best bosses and mentors, COL David Biscomb and COL John Braun, made this point clear to me. If they work for you, they told me, they are yours. If something good happens, it is your fault; if something bad happens, it is your fault.

TP: If you (collectively speaking of you and your people) do good work, then you get the credit. If the work is bad, you will, most assuredly, get the blame.

Leaders have an inherent responsibility to lead the way, literally speaking, in change management. Now let me be very clear that change MUST occur in people and in organizations. We simply must continue to get better than we were. This means the leader must communicate a shared purpose and garner buy-in from the people. People, like organizations, are getting better or getting worse. Getting smarter or getting dumber about work. No one really stands still. People must continue to strengthen their brand. Leaders must seek out potential problems rather than waiting for them to appear. Leaders must be aware of employee complacency and apathy regarding problem management and positively address problems as they arise. Problems will not get better but they can become larger.

---

TP: The leader's purpose is to lead followers, solve problems, perform the mission, and complete the vision.

---

My definition of leadership is that "Leadership is the art of influencing and enabling others to successfully accomplish the requirements of the organization on behalf of the customers and stakeholders" (McGuire, 2007).

It is important to note the significant differences between Management and Leadership. While the differences have been discussed by many authors, I have summarized the comparisons to assist in your cognitive understanding as this understanding is essential to your success as a Leader.

The first comparison by Northouse (2007) suggests **Management produces order and consistency and Leadership produces change and movement. Take a look at the next chart and think about the differences the author has described. Do you agree with his listing?**

## A Comparison of Management and Leadership Competencies

*Source: Northouse, 2007, p.10.*

| Management Produces Order & Consistency | Leadership Produces Change & Movement |
|---|---|
| Planning and Budgeting | Establishing Direction |
| Establishing agendas | Creating a vision |
| Setting timetables | Clarifying the big picture |
| Allocating resources | Setting strategies |
| Organizing and Staffing | Aligning People |
| Provide structure | Communicating goals |
| Making job placements | Seeking commitment |
| Establishing rules and procedures | Building teams and coalitions |
| Controlling and Problem Solving | Motivating and Inspiring |
| Developing incentives | Inspiring and energize |
| Generating creative solutions | Empowering subordinates |
| Taking corrective action | Satisfying unmet needs |

As shown in the next table, there are distinct differences between Leadership and Management (Bennis, 1989). I would like to add some narrative between my own experiences and the original list from Bennis.

The first and third columns are the original list from Bennis and the second and fourth are my additions based upon my experience and research.

## Differences between Leadership and Management, Bennis, 1989 and McGuire, 2012

| Leadership (Bennis) | Leadership (McGuire) | Management (Bennis) | Management (McGuire) |
|---|---|---|---|
| Innovation | Must innovate; lead the way with deliberate and intentional change | Administration | Care about continuing what we are doing; Stay the same; Fights innovation and any change |
| Original | Seem crazy at times; future oriented; <u>does not</u> follow current procedures blindly | Copy of others | Follow the organization models previously shown; follows procedures blindly |
| Develops | Develops people and the organizational mission; encourages others | Maintains | Maintains status quo and fights to prevent compliments to others |
| Focuses on the people | Looks at strengths and opportunities for employees | Focuses on systems and structures | Looks for systems to improve the organization |

| | | | |
|---|---|---|---|
| Inspires Trust | Works to build relationships | Relies on Control | Uses fear as a key management tool |
| Long-range perspective | Concerned about 3-5 years in the future | Short-range view of actions | Concerned about today and this week |
| Asks what and why | What do you want and why do you want it; why is a key response for innovation | Asks how and when | How do you want it and when do you want it; status quo; never questioning why |
| Eye on the horizon and beyond | Concerned about today but more concerned about 3 years from now | Eye on the bottom line | Concerned about day-to-day operations only; impact for today? |
| Challenges the status quo | Asks why; searches for root causes of problems; deeper looks | Accepts the status quo | Not overly concerned with anything but today and this week |
| Crazy at times | Appears to be insane in individual improvements; has mentors; reads; explores regularly | Stays in line | Does not stray from established work or procedures; superficial; no mentors; relies on self |

| Does the right thing | Works the most important priorities of the organization | Does things right | Works as directed; does not address priorities; works what is next |
|---|---|---|---|
| Heart (emotions) | Work with heart of employees; emotional | Head (thinking) | Work with head and do not care about emotions |

One of my favorite authors on leadership, Fred A. Manske, Jr. sees leadership a little differently than Bennis or Northouse. Manske (1999, p. 7) has a chart with his leadership attributes and I have taken the opportunity to add some comments as noted below. I am in agreement with Manske for the most part but want to add my illumination based on my experiences and research.

| Leaders Tend to (Manske, 1999) | Leaders Tend to (McGuire) | Managers Tend to (Manske, 1999) | Managers Tend to (McGuire) |
|---|---|---|---|
| Stress relationships with others, values and commitment | No excuses type of environment; relationship building is important; Trust driven | Stress organization, coordination and control | Believe deeply in the system and the policies and procedures; do the same tomorrow; Fear driven |

| | | | |
|---|---|---|---|
| Create and articulate a vision for the long run | Accomplish strategic planning and actually follow it; short and long term goals | Focus on achievement of short term objectives/goals | Live in the present; worry about today and this week |
| Empower people to act independently | Be good teachers and communicators | Insist on people checking in with them before action | Work on controlling every aspect of work/people |
| Favor taking risks/changes | Understand change is constant | Fear uncertainty and act cautiously | Worry about bottom line to the exclusion of the people |
| Generate a feeling of meaning | Link everyone together and team build | Enforce fulfillment of agreements and contracts | Worry about controlling work and people |
| Think strategically | Look into the future state | Seldom think strategically | Worry about short term only |
| Insatiable passion to continually develop | Continually learning with mentors, books, research | Not to push themselves to learn new things | Think that they know all they need to know |

*Chart adapted from Manske (1999, p. 7) and Dr. McGuire's (2012) work*

Other well-known authors, Kouzes and Posner (1987), indicate successful leaders challenge the process, inspire a shared vision, enable others to act, model the way, and encourage the heart.

In conclusion, it should be obvious that there is a significant difference between Management and Leadership. Leadership is much more difficult primarily because of the need to develop deeper relationships in order to propel the organization forward toward a dedicated vision for success.

---

**TP:** It is clear from the above charts and discussions there is a difference between Management and Leadership. Leadership is much harder to accomplish and requires building of relationship and trust with employees and supervisors alike.

---

# Leadership Questions

**Question: Is Leadership more effective than Management?**

Answer: There are literally hundreds of studies about Leadership versus Management and which is more effective. I think to sum all of those studies up, I would say that neither is the best without both being used. Most textbooks used in my MBA classes imply that we need both Management and Leadership but are clear in that Leadership is more difficult to attain. As you will see in this book, Leadership requires deeper relationships and that one aspect suggests Leadership is more difficult to grasp.

I humbly recommend that you look at the lists shown above and self-evaluate where you are in comparison to the narrative. Management is easier due to the shallowness of relationships. Management is necessary to get the job done and is inherently short range primarily. Leadership is more about relationships and selecting a longer term path while not losing sight of the short range.

Therefore, in my opinion, one is not more effective than another to be successful. It depends upon the organization, the experience of the employees, the maturity of the mission, and the capability and capacity of the Leader.

# CHAPTER 1 – TRUST.

## BUILD TRUSTING RELATIONSHIPS THROUGH A DEDICATED VISION.

---

"The best way to find out if you can trust somebody is to trust them."
—*Ernest Hemingway*

"To be trusted is a greater compliment than being loved."
—*George MacDonald*

"Strong, compelling leadership is at the root of all great accomplishments and a lot of routine work. Leaders create follower attitudes that allow them to trust their leaders. Trust is at the root of all great leadership. Leadership and trust have a unique relationship; one means little without the other." —*M. Martin*

"In my humble opinion, Trust is the beginning and ending of any great and worthwhile relationship. Trust is essential in developing followers for any leader." —*C. U. (Mac) McGuire III*

While this chapter may appear to be addressing two disparate topics, let me assure you it is not. The two components – trusting relationships and a dedicated vision – are intertwined. It has been my experience that many leaders lack the capability and capacity to build trusting relationships around a dedicated vision. Trusting relationships are defined as those relationships where Leaders and employees are loyal to each other as well as the organizational priorities. The dedicated vision is defined as a clear direction for the organization with clear priorities for work. When the vision is fully explained with clarity and all subsequent questions are addressed, trusting relationships should be stronger. Let's discuss each one separately and then talk about how they are related.

First, in order to truly build trusting relationships, the Leader must have a full understanding of mission requirements and really comprehend the work of subordinates. The Leader should know the people they work with, understand who they are (capability and capacity), where the Leader wants to go in the organization, where the employees want to go (promotion possibilities or not) in the organization, while keeping Leader/Employee personal goals ever-present in their mind.

Trust takes time and experience. Leaders must build trust in a deliberate and intentional manner one step at a time. There are no shortcuts in building trust. Positive experiences between you and the employees develop trust; negative experiences destroy trust. Once trust has been destroyed, it takes a monumental effort to reinstate it. Destroyed trust ruins relationships. Mutual trust allows the Leader and the subordinate to be solidly connected to accomplishment of organizational and individual goals (dedicated vision).

---

**TP: In order to build positive relationships and get quality work accomplished in a timely manner, trust is a major contributing factor.**

---

Secondly, a dedicated vision (clear direction/purpose for you in the organization with measures) for your life and for the organizational life is indispensable to your success. You must not toil in a position that does not maximize your contribution and/or lead you away from that which you were designed. You need to visualize the manager (leader; my addition of leader) that you want to become (Arvin, 2008). You must tell your employees where the organization is going and allow them to provide input (acquire buy in from them) when and where possible about their concerns, problems, and possible innovation (thoughts) in the organizational journey.

In the book, *Why People Fail,* Reynolds (2012) asserts that an unclear purpose is a major cause of failure in people. It is very difficult to be successful in building a trusting relationship if you do not know the purpose/vision of where you are going and where the organization is going. Reynolds states that many people do not have a vision for their lives much less the purpose/vision of the organization or the people they supervise. An old idiom applies here that sometimes your actions are so loud (you are not walking your talk); I cannot hear your words (about walking your talk). In simpler terms, you must do what you say you will do every day and your people and superiors are watching to verify your words. It is not good to say what you will do and then not do that very thing. Be very careful here in this effort!

---

**TP: You must have a vision (in writing) for your life and for the organization in which you work. Explain it clearly to your people and constantly communicate it with words and actions.**

---

I truly believe the highest compliment a Leader can receive is a compliment given by a subordinate. When you receive compliments from your employees, it generally indicates they understand your definition (purpose/vision) of the organizational requirements and are ready to follow your Leadership. It could indicate they will perform over and above their required job description and will use their own innovation to improve work. This innovation, dare I say, entrepreneurship, is essential to task accomplishment and organizational success. The only real competitive advantage any organization has is the development of their people to address the future.

**TP: The highest compliment for a Leader is one given by their employees.**

In order to have trusting relationships and be able to fully develop your dedicated vision, Leaders must be found to be trustworthy. It is a character trait that must be given before it can be received. Read that last line again. There are a number or character traits that must be given BEFORE they can be received. Some time ago, I visited with a CEO of a major hospital system. The CEO told me he does not fully trust his key Leaders. My response was simple . . . "Trust is a two-way street and he must give it before he can get it" (do not get into the old mindset of saying "trust must be earned"). Be very clear on this, if this CEO does not trust his people, you can be confident that his people do not trust them.

**TP: Trust must be reciprocal! If you cannot give it, then you will never receive it. Trust is the key building block of relationships anywhere and anytime.**

A key part of building trust and defining the dedicated direction for the organization is maintaining your emotional intelligence and emotional control. For the purposes of this book, emotional intelligence refers to the ability to think when problems arise and work the problem wisely. Emotional control refers to the ability to maintain your composure when others are not or when situations cause heightened emotions to become activated in solving problems.

Emotional intelligence (thinking) and emotional control (maintaining composure) can be a very hard lesson to learn. If you are prone to "blow-up" when problems arise, people will normally distance themselves from you. The end result will be a forfeiture of influence by you as the Leader. People will find it difficult to trust you if you are inconsistent in your behavior – positive one day and negative the next or positive one moment on one problem and negative the next moment. People need consistency of emotions! Goleman (2006) in his book about emotional intelligence and its function in the workplace, noted the necessity for Leaders to maintain their emotions and think factually about problems. In Chapter 4, Goleman discusses a story concerning the need for Leaders to know themselves and their feelings. Emotional intelligence and control of those feelings can greatly accelerate relationship building.

---

**TP: Emotional intelligence and control is a necessary ingredient if you want people to trust and follow you.**

---

In summation, trusted leaders (Galford & Drapeau, 2002) tend to free people, fuel passions, provide focus, foster innovation, give the right time for work, lower costs, are contagious, and retain great employees (p. 8-16).

# CHAPTER 1
# QUESTIONS AND ANSWERS

**Question: How is the best way to build trust?**

There are seven ways that I have found to build trust in the workplace.

1. Be authentic. Don't try to be anyone else. Be sincere and treat <u>everyone</u> with respect and dignity. This would include your boss, your employees, peers, and to the people working in lower positions of your organization. Everyone!

2. Believe all employees want to do a good job. There are a number of research articles suggesting that almost every employee wants to do a good job when they come to work – not a bad job. Treat them as though you know they only do great work.

3. Communicate frequently. Make sure you are spending time with your people to fully understand their problems and concerns. Talk to them often and let them know the value they provide to you and the organization by their dedication and loyalty.

4. Terminate bad employees. This may sound unusual but you must get rid of those employees who refuse to focus on the organizational vision or improve their work skills. It assures the good employees that you appreciate them and have high

expectations for all employees. Do not make the mistake of reassigning work from a bad employee to a hard working employee.

5. Illuminate team goals as well as individual ones. Make sure everyone knows their role and what the goals are for the organization and each employee.

6. Act and be consistent. It will help build trust if the employees can count on you to do what you say you will do.

7. Be honest. Tell them the truth about the organization and their individual work. This honesty may need to be tempered with the approval of what your supervisors say you can discuss. Be transparent to the maximum extent possible (office policy/procedures) and tell your employees as much you can.

**Question: What can you do when you have lost trust in your boss for whatever reason? What can you do when you have lost trust in one of your employees? What can you do when your boss or employees have lost trust in you?**

I put all of these scenarios in the same question because the answer is the same. This trust deficit occurs in situations where you have spent a long time together and you know each other's faults. There is but one way I have found to handle this scenario. In the case of losing trust in your boss, you must go to the boss and tell them you realize your mistake. Additionally, explain to the boss that you intend to redouble your efforts to do a better job in trusting them. This is very difficult to do but necessary to wipe the board clean and start anew.

In the scenario where you have lost trust in one of your employees, you will have to go to that employee and tell them about the loss of trust. Ask them to redouble their efforts to reinitiate the trust needed to make work successful.

In the third scenario where your boss and employees may have lost trust in you, you will need to go to them individually and tell them about the belief that there is some lost trust and that you are redoubling your effort to reinstate the trust needed for successful work.

Notice I put the action squarely in your corner. You must act! This problem will not, repeat not, get better with time but will probably get much worse.

The strongest person wipes the slate clean and begins again. Someone must be the strong person and that would be you since you are reading this book. But a slate cleaning is needed at least every two or three years at a minimum. Perhaps more frequent depending on the organization. The longer we work together, the more I can see your faults, your problems, and your weaknesses. People seem to harbor wrongs done to them (their perception). This familiarity leads to contempt. The longer we work together the more you can upset me and the more I will have to forgive you and vice versa.

**Question: Does building trust take time or can it be built quickly?**

The length of time it takes to build trust depends upon the people involved and their commitment to making trust a part of the relationship. There is no magical period of time but most will say it takes several years to fully develop trust. Relationships routinely take time and trust is a byproduct of the relationship.

# Chapter 2 – Teambuilding.

## Build an effective team of individuals by inspiring and energizing them to perform at their best; Leaders really appeal to hearts (motivation) and not minds.

---

"Coming together is a beginning. Keeping together is progress. Working together is success." —*Henry Ford*

"We must all hang together, or assuredly, we shall all hang separately." —*Benjamin Franklin*

"Leadership: The art of getting someone else to do something you want done because he wants to do it." —*Dwight D. Eisenhower*

"A team is a group of individuals that band together to accomplish organizational requirements. They forgo their individual needs/concerns for the sake of mission accomplishment." —*C. U. (Mac) McGuire III*

I personally believe that before you can become a supervisor of anyone – you must have a certificate in your file stating you have been a head coach or assistant coach in T-ball baseball for at least two years. Those 5 and 6 year old youngsters will do exactly what you say and play exactly how you played in practices. What a frustrating time when those youngsters do exactly what you said and not what you meant. T-ball experience (when you finish it) will teach you how to train others, give you great insight on your communication skills, and will help you deal with your emotional intelligence and control referred to in the previous chapter.

I have so many, many stories about my T-ball experiences. One evening before the game as I was standing in the outfield (in T-ball, a coach can stand in the outfield during the game to direct traffic) a young man (age 5) came to tell me he needed to go to the bathroom. I told him we had some time so "GO." He did "Go" as I told him but it was against the fence in the outfield. As I was focused on positioning an additional outfielder, another youngster ran up to me and told me "Johnny is peeing on the fence." When you hear that, you immediately panic because you, in your heart of hearts, know it is true. These young children will almost always tell you the truth. I walked over to Johnny (name changed for obvious reasons) and told him that I meant for him to go to the restroom behind the concession stand. He looked up at me, still peeing, and his exact words were – "You didn't say that!" And . . . I did not. It was my fault for not being clear with my guidance. Sometimes we blame others when it is our fault.

That would be a great lesson if that were the end. It wasn't. I looked up and here comes Johnny's mother who appeared really upset. I met her at the foul line and made a startling revelation to her again showing my excellent communication skills. I told her that the event (Johnny peeing on the fence) was my fault. To which she glared at me and asked me if I had told Johnny to pee on the fence. Am I in trouble because of my poor communication? I told her what I had said and I took full responsibility for the problem trying to get Johnny off the hook since I felt badly for him and my now obvious inability to direct him properly. She calmed down and I walked back to my place in the outfield. Another lesson learned about Leadership and communication. The story could end here but I should probably tell you the "rest of the story." When I told Johnny that I thought his mother was really upset, he shared that his dad, his little brother, and himself pee in the back yard all the time so it was really not a big deal. I remained silent after this startling discovery but often wondered if that practice by the males in his family continued after this event.

---

**TP: Be very careful what you say and how you act around your team. Be very, very clear about what you want and what you need. Assume your communication will not be understood the first time.**

---

In order to build an effective team, you need to consider the following:

1. A vision of what the team must accomplish. You must attempt to build "cohesiveness and pride" (Manske, 1990, p. 25) at the same time. They must feel as one unit. The fuel of organizations is pride and a sense of accomplishment.

2. A mission that can be accomplished. The team will have to coalesce around a mission, which is realistic, measurable and attainable.

3. Great hiring process. You must take your time to find the best and brightest people for your organization. You must also look for capacity and capability gaps in your current team. Do we need someone good with numbers? Do we need someone who can accomplish strategic planning? Hire very carefully and try to always hire someone smarter than you. Remember to consider versatility in your hiring practices. Do we have someone who can fill multiple positions if needed?

4. Train the employees. Training of the employees is critical once in the organization. Orientation is the time to set the culture in the mind of the employee which will guide all work and decisions.

5.  Provide accurate job descriptions. Make sure the employee knows, without a shadow of a doubt, exactly what they will be evaluated on in the performance review.

6.  Evaluate appropriately. Leaders must ensure that personnel evaluations are candid and honest. Leaders must evaluate each employee with clarity based on the mission and job description. Changes/revisions to job requirements may be necessary based upon organizational needs.

---

**TP: In other words, find your gaps (job/task shortcomings in your organization) and fill them with the best available people. Everyone, and I do mean everyone, wants to be on a successful (winning) team.**

---

Let me now share stories from a number of Leaders who have left behind legacies and lessons that we all can use to help us become great Leaders. Mother Teresa was a diminutive Albanian nun who decided at an early age to go India and serve the poor the rest of her life. She stepped in the slums of Calcutta to live amongst the poorest of the poor (Spink, 1997). Spink includes in her book some of Mother Teresa's philosophy of life that "life is an opportunity, avail it, life is a beauty, admire it, and life is a dream, realize it" (p. xiv). Her love of her savior, Jesus Christ, led her to build a very successful team to care for the sick and poor. She solicited/selected other team members to come along side and work hard with her. She labored for over 30 years before receiving notoriety for her work and won the Nobel Peace Prize in 1979. In 1999, she was one of the most admired people of the 20th century in a US poll. At the time of her death, her order operated 610 missions in 123 countries. She was able to motivate a great number of people to her cause carefully choosing those people with a similar passion.

TP: Build your team carefully. Others should be encouraged to come along side you. Look for those with a passion first.

Another great team Leader was George Bush Sr. (President Number 41) according to General Colin Powell (2003) in his book *My American Journey*. Although General Powell was not the most senior officer, President Bush carefully selected him for the position as the senior military leader (Chairman, Joint Chiefs of Staff). Bush assembled a great team around Powell and in his book; Powell recounts a number of times where President Bush supported him even when General Powell had made a mistake. All members of the team knew President Bush was in charge but they also knew he listened to his team when making critical decisions.

TP: Assemble your team and listen to them. Treat each member of your team with respect and dignity.

Leaders at all levels must provide direction about priorities and time needed, resources to get the job done, and finally, application of the talent of the organization on the most difficult tasks. Your best people must be working on your most difficult organizational tasks.

TP: You can be the Leader and still listen to the team for advice.

In my classes in corporate America, at the University of Texas Professional Development Center, and in the classes at the University of Mary Hardin Baylor MBA Program, I am often asked about how a Leader can motivate employees. I have found in my life journey that there are eight key ways to motivate others.

✓ <u>The Leader must be inspired by life</u> – Are you inspired each day by the day itself and what it may bring? You must be energized and excited about your work and your life. Your past cannot be brighter than your future or you are in a rut. My grandmother said a rut is a grave with both ends hollowed out. Don't get in a rut or allow circumstances to bring you down. One of my favorite books is Victor Frankl's (1959) *Man's Search for Meaning*. Before the war, Frankl had two doctorates in medicine and philosophy. He was in a concentration camp in World War II. He labored there and saw many of his family killed. He saw beauty in having a shoestring when others did not. He pictured himself in a faraway place – away from this deprivation. He even saw a reason to live in a concentration camp. If he can do that, you can be inspired by the day and your work. Count your blessings every day. If you are inspired and motivated by life, then others can inspire and motivate others.

✓ <u>The Leader must be emboldened and purposeful by short and longer term goals</u>. The Leader needs a Personal Strategic Plan (PSP) congruent with the Organizational Strategic Plan (OSP) or PSP=OSP. Wilson & Dobson (2008) on pages 4-9 share ten guidelines for personal goals. If the OSP is not in line with your PSP, you may be in the wrong organization and wasting time. The Leader must see opportunities each day to make a difference in short term and longer-term goals – organizational and personal. If you have goals and are motivated to achieve them, then you can assist others with their goals.

✓ <u>The Leader must develop networks with positive people</u>. Let me emphasize the criticality of being around positive people. If you can't get that interaction at work, you must seek out others who can give you an optimistic view of life.

✓ <u>Leaders must be able to give rewards/praise for good work</u>. There is a necessity to be acknowledged at work and at home. Without this appreciation, we all will lose sight of why we are here in the first place. DeVos (2008) outlines the ten most powerful phrases for positive people in his book which I recommend reading. Phrases like "I'm wrong", "I'm sorry", and "I believe in you", are but some of those needed phrases. Thomas (2009) published a very good list of extrinsic and intrinsic rewards for the work environment. Website at http://www.iveybusinessjournal.com/topics/the-work-place/the-four-intrinsic-rewards-that-drive-employee-engagement. In praising employees, I like the suggestions of Haden (2012) which lists 9 elements of highly effective employee praise on a website address http://www.inc.com/jeff-haden/the-9-elements-of-highly-effective-employee-praise.html. By praising others when justified, motivation will follow. Therefore the key to motivation is justified, intentional praise about a specific event.

✓ Leaders must accomplish physical exercise. I know this is difficult in the press of daily life but it is a necessity for your health and for your ability to get work done as it assists with the connection of mind to the body. The Mayo Clinic completed a study where they proved physical exercise will help you feel better (after the soreness goes away). Exercise controls weight, combats health conditions/diseases, improves mood, boosts energy, promotes better sleep, puts extra spark in your sex life, and can be fun (not sure about the last one?). Thirty minutes per day is suggested by the study but even every other day is helpful. Website for the study is http://www.mayoclinic.com/health/exercise/HQ01676/NSECTIONGROUP=2. If you feel good about your general health, you are motivated to conquer your work and help others.

✓ Leaders must be good at time management. We must simply stay whelmed; not overwhelmed or underwhelmed – but whelmed. Stay balanced in your life between work, personal lives, and what you like to do.

✓ <u>Leaders need to take time for recreation and leisure</u>. There is a necessity for time off from work – dedicated time. A good website for planning leisure time and how it is defined can be found at http://www.laynetworks.com/MANAGING-LEISURE-TIME.html. Time off will help to clear the mind and can contribute to personal motivation after short periods away from work. The Leader must judiciously decide when to be away and it cannot be when you may be needed for actions related to the strategic plan. As an example, a superintendent cannot leave the school for recreation when essential student testing is underway.

✓ <u>Leaders need to find mentors.</u> Bell (2002) suggests mentors can be your manager or leader, and they can motivate you if you know they care about your success. One word of caution here, I have had very little success being honest with my bosses/superiors and them not using it against me later. To have a true mentoring relationship requires honesty and this makes the workplace a problem. Most of my best mentors came from outside the workplace to allow them to be totally honest with me without having the personalities at my work to consider. Mentoring can be done by informal (asking for help sometime) to formal (requiring a document of improvement from mentor to mentee) per website http://www.opm.gov/hrd/lead/BestPractices-Mentoring.pdf. Selecting the right mentor can be motivating as you will learn that most of your problems have been dealt with before.

---

TP: You must take time for organizing your life. Being whelmed allows the Leader to focus on the most important priorities.

---

# CHAPTER 2
# QUESTIONS AND ANSWERS

**Question: What if the team you are on was not built carefully and is not very effective?**

Answer: This is a common concern. Often, people are hired independently of what the organization really needs. It appears most organizations look deeply into an applicant's individual skills without much consideration of how those skills fit with organizational needs. Leaders know that taking time to select the right person with the right skill sets for the right job is a hit and miss proposition. So, we routinely do not take the time to make the best decision for the organization as a whole. Your job as an effective Leader is to make sure additions to your team are hired based on how they can help the team meet the long term goals of the organization. Establish some quantitative (well-defined) and qualitative (open-ended) questions.

**Question: How do you motivate yourself when you are not on an effective team?**

Answer: Great question! I have had to negotiate this task of being on a team or leading a team that I was not involved in putting together. There are four things you must do.

1. Understand the mission of the team. Sometimes I could not get motivated to make a difference because I did not understand what we were doing, why or how we should do it.

2. Get a great mentor to help you deal with problems that arise. As discussed previously, I recommend that this mentor be from outside of the organization for the best results. The mentor can be someone you can lean on to help make the best decisions possible.

3. Model the appropriate behavior for your team. This is critical. Your team needs to know your expectations and what "good" work looks like.

4. Finally, choose to have a positive attitude! When I complained about the first grade and how hard it was my grandmother said, "You need to get happy in the same pants you got mad in." That phase has stuck with me when I did not find myself in the best organizations or with the best boss. The Leader must understand they must choose to have a positive attitude, even in trying times. A positive attitude can make a significant difference in the life of the Leader and in the life of people who depend on the Leader . . . both at work and at home.

**Question: How can I possibly find time to exercise and eat right?**

Answer: This is another great question that most all of us have wrestled with from time to time or soon will. The age of the Leader will have an impact on the type of exercise and how frequently it should be done. When I was younger, I did not need to be as deliberate (regular schedule) about exercising but later in life have found exercising to be very important in maintaining my health. There is simply one answer to this question about finding time – make it a priority in your life. Make plans with your family and make it a joint effort.

This will encourage family time and better health. That's it! If it is a priority, you will get it done. As has been mentioned earlier in this book, the Mayo Clinic http://www.mayoclinic.com/health/exercise/HQ01676/ lists seven benefits of a regular physical activity plan:

1.  exercise controls weight,

2.  combats health conditions/diseases,

3.  improves mood,

4.  boosts energy,

5.  promotes better sleep,

6.  puts extra spark in your sex life, and,

7.  can be fun (not sure about this one?)

# CHAPTER 3 – EXHIBIT HONESTY AND INTEGRITY.

---

"No legacy is so rich as Honesty." —*William Shakespeare*

"Always tell the Truth. That way, you don't have to remember what you said." —*Mark Twain*

"Honesty is the first chapter in the book of wisdom." —*Thomas Jefferson*

"Integrity is doing the right thing, even if nobody is watching." —unknown author

"Integrity is telling myself the Truth. And Honesty is telling the Truth to other people." —*Spencer Johnson*

"Real integrity is doing the right thing, knowing that nobody's going to know whether you did it or not." —*Oprah Winfrey*

Honesty is defined by dictionary.com (http://dictionary.reference.com/browse/honesty?s=t) as "the quality or fact of being honest; uprightness and fairness; truthfulness, sincerity, or frankness; freedom from deceit or fraud." I might add straightforward in conduct; consistent. We need to be honest with our people and with ourselves. I used to hate it when my superiors would tell me to withhold essential information that could help us communicate with our people. In fact, I resented keeping secrets from my people when the information could help them. You may have to deal with those secrets as well in your Leadership positions. My advice is to be as honest as you can be within your circumstances knowing that dishonestly can have a negative impact on the organization.

If you really want to gain the highest level of respect and have the people follow you, you must exhibit honesty and integrity with customers, superiors, suppliers, partners, collaborators and employees at all times. If you are in a school setting, you need to exhibit honesty and integrity with everyone including students, parents, staff, and community members. If in a hospital or medical facility, you must exhibit honesty and integrity with patients, family members, and staff. In a business, Leaders need to display honesty and integrity with customers and employees alike. Based upon my experience, there are and will be opportunities at work to lie, cheat, or be dishonest with others. You should never get caught in a situation where you attempt to justify dishonest actions as a solution to a problem. You must stay above it.

Leaders always provide accurate information as they know it. The truth can be elusive and time related. In my military days, I would give orders or information to my soldiers and civilian employees based upon what I knew at the time the orders were given. I would insert the time (Example: 1600 hours) because sometimes plans had to be changed by the minute. If I gave an order and it was changed moments later, I did not want it to appear as though I had lied. It can be difficult to communicate changes quickly to all your people, so have a process in place to ensure that they know changes are based on circumstances and new information instead of dishonesty.

**TP: Being honest at all times is critical to gaining trust. Honesty can appear to be elusive at times from different perspectives.**

Integrity is defined by dictionary.com (http://dictionary.reference.com/browse/integrity?s=t) as "adherence to moral and ethical principles; soundness of moral character; honesty; the state of being whole, entire, or undiminished; a sound, unimpaired, or perfect condition." As you can tell by the difficult definition, this will be hard work throughout your life. Integrity encompasses so many aspects of work. With ethics as a critical underpinning, integrity will need to be monitored by the Leader constantly.

Modeling integrity is sometimes more difficult. The integrity of the Leader, like trust, is under constant review. Will you do the right thing? Once an employee told me that a vendor had paid us twice for a product. The employee was laughing and enjoying the fact that due to the error by the vendor we would have a budget surplus. I told my employee to call the vendor and tell them about the problem. My employee thought it would be okay to take the double payment since it was the mistake of the vendor. I informed him that we needed to do what was right by every vendor. Integrity and honesty never, and I do mean never, take a day or moment off. Leaders must always do the right thing!

**TP: Your integrity is on display every day in every situation. Make sure you make the right choices.**

Followers want standards. What are standards of work? Most often I define it as levels of performance which may include requirements or expectations of each job task. In layman's terms, the minimum job requirements. People in the workforce need these standards setting the minimum level of work. More information can be found at http://www.opm.gov/perform/wppdf/handbook.pdf.

To achieve a high quality organization, the highest standards must be applied to every circumstance. It can be much easier for you to take the easy way out. However, it will not pay off in the end! Although a decision may appear to be easier, dishonesty and a lack of integrity will ultimately create insurmountable problems for you and the organization. As an example, I once had an employee who asked me to falsify (sign documents) physical training requirements for him. He was an outstanding employee, and I truly did not want to lose his expertise in my organization. However, I knew that falsifying records even one time was dishonest, reflected a lack of integrity on my part, and was a drop in our organizational standards. While he could have made a choice to obtain a release from a doctor to modify his physical requirements (standard process), he chose not to do that. This put me in the awkward position of lying (by signing the documents) for him or doing the right thing which ultimately cost him his job. I hope you never have to make this type of tough choice. Someone may ask you to be dishonest, drop organizational standards, or make poor choices. My recommendation to you is that the right choice should always be your choice. It leads to truth, honesty, and high standards of integrity.

---

**TP: Honesty and high integrity are necessary. Standards must be carefully established. They must not be moved or comprised for anyone, including the Leaders.**

---

Let me end this chapter by saying being honest with someone is often hard to do as the truth often hurts. To tell the truth is being honest and reflects your integrity with others. I therefore admonish you to tell the truth and be honest with those around you at all times.

One caveat that I would like to share however is that, I have had bosses in the past who really did not want to hear the truth about them, the organization, or the staff. Be very careful and seek out guidance from your mentors in those circumstances. In these circumstances, the truth may not be acceptable and you may be forced to make a hard decision up to and including seeking other employment. Be prepared for that consequence!

---

**TP: Being honest and showing integrity is often harder than you think but will help you and the organization in the long run.**

---

We can be honest without being mean. I think it has to do with your heart and how you approach others. If you really intend for your honesty to be instructive and you do not have an ulterior motive, you can be honest without being brutal or attacking the other person. Remember if you treat everyone with respect and dignity, your honest comments will be easier to deliver and will enlighten others in a positive way.

---

**TP: You do not have to be mean and spiteful to be honest. You will need to establish a reputation for telling the truth in order to be received well by others.**

---

# CHAPTER 3
# QUESTIONS AND ANSWERS

**Question: What if there are little or no standards at work? How can you instill them?**

You will have to evaluate where the organization is and start small. I recommend drafting a list of initial steps to set standards for submission to your boss for approval. The boss may make some changes, which is ok as long as you have not compromised too much. If the boss refuses to set the standards at all, look to move to another position within the organization or float your resume in your networks. Major problems will be forthcoming if no there are no standards and you do not want to be there when that happens.

**Question: What should you do if your boss is not honest most of the time?**

This is a real problem and can lead to problems with the people you supervise. You must stay the course and try to remain above the dishonest actions of your superior. Do not make the mistake of thinking it is okay to lie in some cases. Two wrongs do not make a right. You must remain honest and truthful at all times.

**Question: What can you do if you have already made some serious mistakes with honesty and integrity?**

Learn from your mistakes. Get help from a mentor. Let everyone know that you have changed or you are working on it. Ask others who are good at this to help you inside your organization. Share with others how this book is helping you grow. Show them your change by your words and by your actions. However, be prepared to be challenged and tested by the worst employees who will try to drag you back to your old ways. Stay the course and do the right things for you, your people, and the organization.

---

TP: Remember to be honest and exhibit integrity toward your boss, peers, and employees. You will be better for it.

---

# CHAPTER 4 – VISION.

## HAVE A VISION OF WHERE YOU NEED TO GO INDIVIDUALLY AND ORGANIZATIONALLY SUPPORTED BY YOUR NEXT LEVEL BOSS. (STRATEGIC PLANNING)

---

"I can teach anybody how to get what they want out of life. The problem is that I can't find anybody who can tell me what they want."
—*Mark Twain*

"It is a terrible thing to see and have no vision."   —*Helen Keller*

"Where there is no vision, there is no hope."
—*George Washington Carver*

"Vision is the direction of your personal or organizational life. Your vision must be in writing and should cause a continual focus on what is right for you and for your organization. Vision is therefore essential for life/work enjoyment."   —*C. U. (Mac) McGuire III*

As is often quoted, "Where there is no vision, the people perish" Proverbs 29:18 http://kingjbible.com/proverbs/29.htm.

I often wonder why so many organizations lack a vision? Why are so many people working where there is no clear direction? How can Leaders possibly expect excellence from their people without a clear path described in the organizational vision? How can you achieve your life goals without a personal vision? The vision is a roadmap for the organization. It is where we are going!

Additional definitions of a vision include:

Kouzes & Posner (1995) "**...an ideal and unique image of the future.**"

Greenleaf (1997) "**...sense of the unknowable and be able to foresee the unforeseeable.**"

Senge (1990) "**...shared vision is vital for ... a learning organization.**"

Many participants in my Leadership classes indicate there is no vision in their organization. They have most often said, there is a complete "lack of direction." There is not a vision or a mission for the organization in their workplace or the vision and mission stated have little or no meaning to anyone. The participants admit to having no idea where the Leaders are trying to take the organization. How tragic?

---

**TP: A vision for the organization in which you lead is critical to outline and show the path to success.**

---

I think Bennis and Nanus (2003) have the best description of an organizational vision stating that the vision should:

- fit the organization,

- set standards for excellence and high ideals,

- clarify the purpose and direction,

- inspires enthusiasm and encourage commitment,

- be well-articulated and easily understood, and,

- be reflective of the organization and its capabilities.

---

TP: Having a vision for the organization helps everyone understand the priorities of work, defines who the customers are, and what is required of employees.

---

The vision of the organization should be clearly communicated well to all concerned. Supervisors need to understand the role they have in the organization and to understand their employee's roles as well. Each employee should know the top three jobs/tasks needed to be accomplished on a regular basis (daily). The employees deserve direction from their supervisors. This will work to align the work with the direction of the organization.

---

TP: Everyone needs to fully understand their role to play in organizational and individual success. If there is no vision for your organization or your position, at a minimum, suggest three priorities to your supervisor for approval.

---

It has been my experience that true Leaders have an organizational strategic plan (OSP) and a matching or congruent personal strategic plan (PSP). Therefore the OSP=PSP. While you may not have control over the organizational strategic plan, you should have a personal strategic plan for your life. Where do you really want to be in five years? Ten years? After you retire from this first life, what do you really want to do and how can positioning in the organization help you?

As an example, the other day a man came to me and said his plan for his future was to teach Information Technology at a community college when he retires from his IT job in five years. When I asked him about his teaching experience, he indicated he had none. I asked him where teaching was done at his current organization. He responded that all training/teaching was done in Human Resources. I promptly suggested he might want to ask for a transfer from IT to HR with the intent of gaining valuable teaching experience so he could prepare himself for his future employment and still help his organization. In order to become a better teacher you have to teach; but teaching more does not make you better unless you grow in your skills and knowledge.

---

TP: Look for ways to move about in your organization to get you ready to highlight your strengths and passion or perhaps prepare you for your next job within the organization. You can prepare yourself for what you want to do while helping the organization at the same time.

---

# CHAPTER 4
# QUESTIONS AND ANSWERS

**Question: What do you do when your boss says everything is a priority?**

This is a problem and often heard in my classes. As stated earlier, come up with a list of three tasks you believe needs to be accomplished each and every day and are aligned with the organizational vision. These should be global in nature such as (1) provide excellent customer service, (2) develop the employees, and (3) manage resources effectively. Put the priorities on a sheet where everyone you work with, including your supervisor, can see. Let everyone know these are your priorities for the organization. Carefully measure your success in these tasks. If you have selected the right ones, you will constantly be working on them. If not, your priorities will be changed by your supervisor. Word of caution here! If your supervisor wants to change priorities every moment of every day, your priorities are of little value. If the supervisor appreciates your list, you will set the stage for others to make a list which will help everyone stay focused on the vision of the organization.

**Question: What if you are not sure where the organization is going and whether it will exist in its current state in the future?**

You will have to take a serious look at where the organization is going in the five/ten/fifteen year timeframe. Are you in an organization with bad Leaders at the top? Do you have an ineffective supervisor? Chances are that when you look deeply at your organization you can either see the future or not. Johnson (1995) suggests we look closely in our organizations to determine if we are just "rearranging chairs on the Titanic." Are we like the band on the Titanic – who played beautiful music while watching the ship sink? Are you working hard but the ship (organization) is still sinking and not becoming successful? It may be time to look for other employment if the organization is not positioning itself for success.

Question: What if you don't know what you want to do later in your personal life?

That is an obvious concern but not to worry as there are a number of ways to get a handle on this. First, assess what you wanted to be early in life. When you were about 18 or 19 years old, what did you want to be? What did your father or mother do? Did that look appealing to you? My father was a teacher/principal in public schools, and my mother worked for the telephone company. Both of my parents spent their lives helping others. I teach because that is my passion, but also, like my parents, I have a deep desire to help others. Secondly, talk to someone who is doing something that interests you. Seek out your passion by discussing the pros and cons of what they are doing and ask probing questions to help you see what their job is like.

Ask questions such as:

Why do you like your job?

What is the best thing about your job? Worst thing?

Why did you choose this job or did the job choose you?

Finally, look for that passion and what is inside of you. What gifts have you been given (we all have some)? Explore your gifts. Talk to your mentors, friends, and confidantes about what they see you doing in the future. Remember: It is your plan so you are the key! You need to be able to answer the questions about **where are you going in five years? Ten years? Fifteen years?**

# CHAPTER 5 – BE ETHICAL.

"To see what is right and not to do it is want of courage." —*Confucius*

"Personal leadership is the process of keeping your vision and values before you and aligning your life to be congruent with them."
—*Stephen Covey*

"In God we trust, all others bring data." —*Dr. W. Edwards Deming*

"It's not hard to make decisions when you know what your values are."
—*Roy Disney*

First let me define ethics. According to dictionary.com, ethics is a system of moral principles; the rules of conduct recognized in respect to a particular class of human action or a particular group http://dictionary.reference.com/browse/ethics.

Are you proud enough to tell your family and friends about decisions you make at work or at home? Is it the right thing to do based upon the organizational values? Does it treat other people honestly? Does this action violate any laws or company policies? These are just some of the questions arising from ethical decision making.

My grandmother used to say that if you think there is something wrong or if you have to pause before making a decision, there is a good chance it may be unethical. I have found this to be very true in my life.

TP: If you have any doubt about whether the decision you plan to make is ethical or not, you may want to take some time with the decision.

As a Leader you must be ever aware of organizational and individual ethics in the decisions you make. You must be cognizant of decisions made that could cause or lead to fraud, waste, abuse, illegal situations, immoral situations, sexual harassment, or unsafe conditions. These particular areas could limit your effectiveness and/or eventually cause your termination or the termination of others. Ignorance will never be an acceptable excuse for violation of these seven areas.

TP: Be cautious, deliberate, and intentional when making decisions.

The Leader needs to ensure that all staff is provided with a basic understanding of organizational ethics policies and procedures on an annual basis. This annual update should include possible problems encountered in the previous twelve months and suspected problems in the next twelve months. Do not let me suggest here that ethical training is to be done only every twelve months. Ethics training, especially on-the-job training, should be provided as necessary or as problems are revealed (immediately). During this ethics training, consequences for failure should be discussed thoroughly along with some case studies about ethical decisions.

TP: Make sure your employees are aware of possible ethics violations and what they look like. Training is a necessary tool to discuss case studies where other organizations have stumbled.

Decisions made by Leaders must be beyond reproach and clearly ethical to avoid customer complaints, employee complaints, and/or violations of organizational policies and procedures. Be confident you are making your decisions based upon the ethical policies and procedures guiding the organization. Exhibit some patience in making difficult decisions and seek guidance to ensure the decision made is the best option for the organization.

I recommend following the model shown below as one that will help you make the best decisions of behalf of the organization.

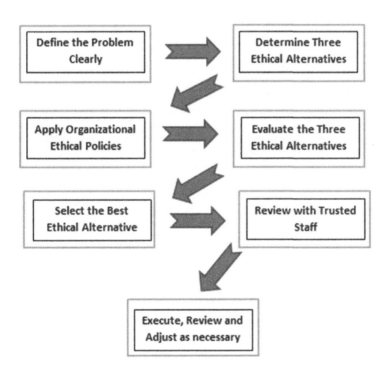

*Ethical Decision Making Model McGuire (2012)*

# CHAPTER 5
# QUESTIONS AND ANSWERS

**Question: What should you do when you know there are unethical activities occurring at work?**

This is a very tough question. My first response is that you need to determine that you know, beyond a shadow of a doubt, that it is unethical or whether you just think it is unethical. Make sure you fully understand the policies and procedures outlining ethical issues where you work. Don't run amok thinking you have unethical issues. Ask questions about how things are going and ask this for clarity from your supervisor. They may be able to guide you. If that is not possible and you suspect they are part of the problem, you will need to consult your mentors about those issues.

If there are unethical issues going on in your organization, follow your policies and procedures to the letter. You also may want to begin a new job search. One of my mentees was working at a Fortune 500 organization where I had previously provided consulting services. She called me late one evening and told me a senior leader requested that she provide an inaccurate report at a meeting the next morning. She was instructed to comply or be terminated. The senior leader had promised a positive report to the CEO and would not back down even though he knew the report was inaccurate and was in violation of company policies. Even though the company had a hotline to report unethical behavior, she was concerned for her job because her boss was very political. She gave the inaccurate report but documented that she was forced to do so. Fortunately, she was able to find other employment quickly but some employees, including her boss, were terminated when the dishonesty was revealed. Always refer to your policies and procedures for guidance regarding decisions being made. Be very careful what you call ethical and unethical on your own.

**Question: In your ethical decision-making model, there are three alternatives. Is this a best practice?**

There are a host of best practices out there. Some work in certain situations better than others. I have found having three alternatives can be beneficial when trying to address decisions that have ethical considerations.

**Question: Can you just stay away from all ethical issues by looking the other way?**

I wish it were that easy. I conducted investigations for the United States Army during one of my assignments. One of the first questions I would ask someone in an investigation about ethical situations was when they first knew there was a problem. If they knew about the issue for more than 24 hours yet did nothing, they became a part of the problem and not the solution. I have seen some people try to plead ignorance but this excuse never works. It is imperative that you make the hard and difficult decision to question the action before it goes too far. Looking the other way simply will not work long term and may not work in the short term either.

# Chapter 6 – Communicate Constantly.

## Work constantly to improve all types of communication with all groups; bosses; peers; and most especially employees.

---

"The single biggest problem in communication is the illusion that it has taken place." —*George Bernard Shaw*

"We have two ears and one mouth so that we can listen twice as much as we speak." —*Epictetus*

"To effectively communicate, we must realize that we are all different in the way we perceive the world and use this understanding as a guide to our communication with others." —*Anthony Robbins*

It is a known fact that employees constantly seek out information and clarity of actions. Leaders or organizations will get the most from their employees by increasing the amount of quality communication that takes place between everyone in the organization.

One way of increasing effective communication is through roundings and more specifically Roundings for Outcomes (RFOs). Leaders must ensure they are conducting RFOs with employees even in remote locations. RFOs occur when the leader circulates amongst the people and inquires about their routines and the type of work they will be doing each day or each week. RFOs are accomplished with a specific purpose in mind and are never haphazard. As an example, Principals/Superintendents need to conduct RFOs with teachers, staff, students, and community leaders. In the medical fields, doctors/nurses/hospital administrators need RFOs with patients, staff, and nurses. Business owners need RFOs with employees and customers. Deliberate questions need to be asked about the vision, mission, values, and goals of the organization. Employees need to be asked about how they are achieving their work on behalf of the organization. RFOs often allow the Leader to identify potential problems BEFORE they develop.

---

**TP: Roundings for Outcomes (RFOs) are critical and recommended to occur throughout the day, including the night shifts. These intentional RFOs should be centered on what everyone is doing to meet or exceed the organizational mission.**

---

If the employees do not get enough information about what is going on to their satisfaction (note to Leaders: to their satisfaction, not yours), they begin to apply their own information and assumptions which could be tragic for work.

---

**TP: Assumptions and bad information can cripple the effectiveness of an organization.**

---

Leaders need to know that often words alone are not sufficient in communication. I once read some research indicating that the 500 most commonly used English words have over 15,000 variations of definitions. Your words and their definitions and my words and my definitions can make communication cumbersome. Using words alone may not be enough to have communication.

Words alone do not always effectively communicate difficult tasks or jobs to others. Visual support (pictures, graphs, charts, tables, etc.) to support what you are trying to say is very important for those who are visual learners. Some of my research indicates over 80% of us are visual learners http://www.visualteachingalliance.com/. Wherever I was a supervisor, I would install a white board in my office and had employees draw and talk about how a particular process should work. This visual aspect along with the words to describe the requirements enhances communication and will help your employees understand their assignments.

---

TP: Visual information (pictures, graphs, charts, tables, etc.) greatly enhances clear communication, and more importantly, clear understanding.

---

Another important tool to improve communication is allowing time for feedback. Feedback allows discussion time to make sure the right message was received. When communicating important information to employees about a job/task, ask the employee to restate back to you the requirements for the task just given to them to check for clarity. Ask the employee to tell you the process they will follow to complete the job/task. Within this discussion dialogue is created, I talk, you listen; you talk, I listen.

One of my friends in the military, Bill Tiemann, used to tell me that dialogue did not begin until we clearly understood each other's point of view. When he explained something to me, I would give him feedback as to what I understood him to say. If he responded with, "we are not having dialogue yet", it let me know I was not receiving his message or he did not understand what I was trying to say. Dialogue occurs when the feedback given agrees with and/or confirms the original instruction given. Therefore, we will have dialogue if the feedback reinforces understanding.

---

TP: Listen to understand what the other person is saying. In my humble opinion, listening is a lost art that is critical to clear communication. Feedback adds clarity. Dialogue (we both talk and listen) is important for both of us.

---

Leaders must give short speeches to the people to rally them around the organizational vision, mission and goals. They deserve it. It does not matter if you are an introvert or an extravert, you must take time to know your people and communicate with them using the dialogue method described above. Complete understanding is needed to achieve organizational goals. Talk to your people to discern what they are doing, determine if it is connected to the vision, mission, and goals, and look for early problems that can be easily resolved.

---

TP: People who work for you are your most important asset and effective communication, feedback, and dialogue are critical for overall organizational success.

---

# CHAPTER 6
# QUESTIONS AND ANSWERS

Question: What does good communication look like?

Wow! Questions keep getting harder. There are five things I recommend.

1.  Take time to really listen to the person talking to you. Listening is an active endeavor. Listen to each word and listen for comprehension

2.  Ask questions for clarity. Ask "why" questions to the person to give you greater insight of their understanding.

3.  Look at the body language and the eyes. Eyes are windows to the soul and can tell you if the person understands and is committed to the ideas presented.

4.  Be "crystal" clear and concise in your communication.

5.  Be patient. Sometimes it takes time to get the general idea of the conversation.

Question: What are some of the types of questions to ask on the Rounding for Outcomes (RFOs)?

At a minimum, you should ask about the vision, mission, and values (Chapter 4). Are the employees on track with measurements? What kind of problems/concerns do they have? How is there attitude? What is the most difficult task you have scheduled for today or this week? Those questions should be addressed in your roundings. I am sure you can think of others.

Question: I have very little extra time, how can you allow time for feedback?

Do you have time to do a job/task several times because the requirements were not clear? Good communication can actually save you time if you are judicious with the time and concise in your dialogue. Leaders need to make sure no time is wasted failing to understand what employees, peers, and supervisors are telling us or trying to tell us.

# CHAPTER 7 – DEVELOP OTHERS.

## ENCOURAGE EMPLOYEES CONTINUALLY AND PUSH THEM IF NECESSARY TO HIGHER LEVELS OF PERFORMANCE.

"All that is valuable in human society depends upon the opportunity for development accorded the individual." —*Albert Einstein*

"If you pick the right people and give them the opportunity to spread their wings—and put compensation as a carrier behind it—you almost don't have to manage them." —*Jack Welch*

"Surround yourself with the best people you can find, delegate authority, and don't interfere as long as the policy you've decided upon is being carried out." —*Ronald Reagan*

This chapter is a lot of fun – work on developing people – is a true passion of mine, and I hope you can grow to enjoy as well. PEOPLE are critical to goal accomplishment! An effective leader must work on developing people beyond their current capabilities and help them be better prepared to accomplish the vision, mission, values, purpose, and goals. Some organizations put these on a card carried by all employees as a reminder of why they are there. Whatever the method, insist that all employees focus on the accomplishment of the vision, mission, values, purpose and goals and encourage them to develop themselves to be able to effectively perform their role.

There are a number of ways to pursue this development of your people but I think the single best way is with a detailed, deliberate Individual Development Plan (IDP). Some organizations use the term Personal Development Plan (PDP). The term you use is not important. However, actually using one of the two is critical.

The major component of the IDP/PDP is candid performance evaluations. Performance evaluations are complicated by the number of employees and the technical nature of their work. As an example, I once had medical units, maintenance units, food service units, and transportation units under my command. Each of those elements had different skill sets and different cultures to deal with. Add to that around 1200 employees and you can begin to see the difficulties. However, it is critical that the utilization of the IDP/PDP permeate the entire organization including the senior Leader. The principle purpose of the IDP/PDP is to make you better for yourself as well as for the organization.

The IDP or PDP should include a section on identifying specific strengths, weaknesses, opportunities and threats/challenges (SWOT/C). The strengths should outline what tasks they do well, weaknesses detailing what tasks they do not do well, opportunities highlight what they need to work on or what education/training they need, and threats/challenges describe what will keep them from being successful.

---

**TP: Each employee that works for you must have an Individual Development Plan (IDP) or Personal Development Plan (PDP) including what needs to be addressed in the short and longer term for the organization and personal success.**

---

As shown in the charts below, Leaders most often do not have an in-depth understanding of what their employees are going through and what they need for their IDP/PDP. Positions within an organization will look differently depending upon your position in the organization. This view is not necessarily right or wrong . . . just different. You should note that your perspective of the organization will change as you are promoted to different positions. Organizationally, we have work to overcome this lack of understanding by constant, candid communication and feedback from each level to the other. Take a look at the charts below and I think you can more clearly understand how Leaders may not cognitively and fully understand their employees.

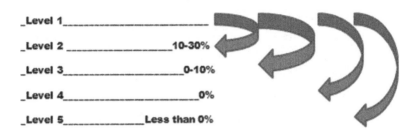

Based upon my research and experience, Level 1 Leaders, CEOs/CIOs/CFOs/Superintendents or EIEIOs (joke here as there are many, many types of O's), know about 10-30% of what is happening below them at Level 2. However, they may believe they know/understand all of it.

Those same Senior Leaders at Level 1 (CEO/CFO/CIO/Superintendents) generally know and understand about 0-10% of what is happening at Level 3. But again, they may perceive they are fully aware of what is happening. It is usually a surprise to them when they find out they do not have a clue about what actually happens at this level in any detail.

At the Level 4 from their senior position (Level 1), they know/understand 0% and lower levels result in less than 0% which is mathematically impossible. The point is this – wherever you are in the organization, you often believe that you have all the answers for all levels when in fact, you do not have the information needed to really know. This is just human nature.

As an example, when I promoted to sergeant in the military, I had seven to nine personnel under my authority. As a soldier (private; lower level), I knew my immediate sergeant did not understand what privates were experiencing even though he had been one previously. He had not been a private (at my level) for over three years and things had changed. He did not understand the life of a private since his move to a higher level. I was convinced that he could do his job better if he would just listen to us (at our level).

Clarity came to me one day when I challenged him and suggested things he should be doing at his level to make things better for all of the privates. Now let me tell you I had never worked at his level, had no idea what it was like but I felt very secure in telling him exactly what he needed to do. Did I mention that he was in his senior position of staff sergeant (one level higher than sergeant for non-military types)? He informed me that he had been given some orders from above and was doing what he was told. I realized that I did not understand what he was told (from higher levels) and he did not understand what we privates were going through. This is the conundrum that all Leaders face and it is hopefully what is depicted in this chart. Wherever we are, we sometimes can get carried away and honestly believe we know everything when in fact we usually only know what is happening at the level where we work.

As I moved into the officer ranks, the lack of understanding was magnified because of additional levels of authority. As I went on to higher levels in the organization, the less I knew what it was like to be a private. I knew I needed to do the best job I could at my level but learned that the best way to address this lack of knowledge was to talk to the other levels beneath me to truly understand their point of view.

In yet another example, I was in charge of the rifle range as a young Captain (now an officer). The range had twenty firing lanes some twenty-five yards apart. The lanes were separated by trees and other vegetation barriers. Each solder had a firing point and an assigned lane to fire into and knock down targets.

One day on the range, there was a private who had not hit any targets (that is very bad; I'm not sure I would want him around me in a fire fight). When I asked him why he had not hit the targets in his assigned lane (assigned lane number seven), he told me that the soldiers in lanes eight, nine, and ten were not following the right process of target acquisition in their lanes. After I clearly communicated that his job was to hit targets in lane seven and that my job was to worry about all of the lanes 1-20, he refocused and began to hit the targets in his lane. I also told him that IF he could hit a target in Lane 8-10, it would not count. The lesson to be learned from this is to stop worrying about those things outside of your lane.

---

TP: Leaders assign "lanes of work" for all of their employees. Make sure your people know which lane (type of work) they are supposed to be doing. Don't let them spend precious time and resources focused on someone else's lane!

---

That information is funny except for what follows. It appears, again based upon my research, that wherever we are in the organization, the people who are just below us and just above us do not know what we are doing. Does this sound familiar? WE know we are ok or do we? Take a look at the chart from the opposite perspective.

__Level 1_____ Less than 0%

__Level 2_____0%

__Level 3_____0-10%

__Level 4_____10-30%

__Level 5_____

If we occupy the Level 5 position, we know/understand about 10-30% of what our boss is going through. We are most often not permitted in their meetings so we really do not understand their requirements. We may think we do but we really don't.

From Level 5 to Level 3, we know about 0-10% of what is going in the organizational lives of those superiors. From Level 5 to Level 2, we are again completely lost regarding the requirements of superiors at that level.

---

**TP: Be very, very careful when you say you have all the answers to help the organization and know what the boss should be doing. Unless you are very good with Extra-Sensory Perception (ESP), there is a very good possibility you are as blind to what is going on above you as they are about what is going on below them. Wherever you are in the organization, there is a very good chance you may not fully understand employees/positions/work in the other Levels.**

---

In working to develop people, you will have to empower them. Empowerment to me simply means involving your subordinates and trusting them to make good decisions and do the right thing. A word of caution about empowerment – make sure you clearly show them what "right" looks like BEFORE you turn the work over to them. This training (showing them what right is) can be accomplished by you or the best employee who has the most knowledge concerning the task/assignment. Empowerment can enable you to work on the more difficult tasks at your Level while the employees are allowed to work at their Level. When empowering, go to the employee's strengths and not their weaknesses. My grandmother (1960) used to say "You will never turn a jackass into a racehorse." Be cautious when assigning jobs/tasks to the right person with the right skills, knowledge, and talent to do the jobs/tasks well. Be careful what you ask people to do on your behalf as well as on the behalf of the organization.

I have tried to place a large amount about empowerment in the table below. The left side addresses the person, their capabilities, and their time with the organization. The Bottom of the Table addresses the type of tasks and the complexity of the tasks. The Empowerment Levels are products of the person and the type of tasks/complexity.

As an example, if you have an employee that has been with your organization for over five years in the same type of work and the Type of Task/Complexity is Not Serious, then the employee is Totally Empowered. In another example, if the employee has been with the organization in the same job work for less than three years and the Type of Task/Complexity is Critical to the Mission, the employee should not attempt to do the work without supervision or not do the work at all without help of some kind. Employees need to understand which box they are working in regarding assignment of work.

| Person Capabilities and Tenure | Task Not Serious; Will not impact Mission | Task Serious; Could impact Mission | Task Critical to the Mission |
|---|---|---|---|
| Very Capable; Veteran Employee; Solid Accomplishments; =5 or >10 years in same job area | Totally Empowered; Allowed to function with little supervision | Post-Approval; Contact Supervisor only when new tasks without guidelines are encountered | Follow standing operating procedures; Guidelines for work |

| | | | |
|---|---|---|---|
| Capable Employee; Some Accomplishments; =3 or >5 years in same job area | Post-Approval; Contact Supervisor only when new tasks without guidelines are encountered | Follow standing operating procedures; Guidelines for work | Pre-Approval; Contact Supervisor when encountering tasks in these areas |
| Employee Not Capable; Few Accomplishments; <3 years in the same job area | Follow standing operating procedures; guidelines for work | Pre-Approval; Contact Supervisor when encountering tasks in these areas | Not empowered; Do not attempt to work those issues in this area without supervision |

*Empowerment Model (McGuire 2012)*

Leaders should ensure that this model is followed and clearly designate where the employee is regarding their capability and the type of tasks to be accomplished. I recommend placing this chart near your office and using this chart to discuss and identify the employee's capability and the difficulty of the task. As an example, a veteran employee can be totally empowered, need post-approval (talk about their decision with the Leader), or follow guidelines if the task is critical to the mission being accomplished. Leaders need to have frank conversations with employees and have the employees point/describe which box they think they are with regard to the intersection of employee capability and type of task/task complexity.

---

TP: When empowering and employee, go to their strengths and avoid their weaknesses when possible. Set them up for success by showing them what right looks like.

---

Positive counseling is another key component for developing your people. Lieutenant Colonel Bill Lee, taught me to be positive in counseling at all times because the outcome must be directed toward improving work.

I like to use the OREO technique. When you identify a problem, find out what really happened. No one knows that event better than the person who was there. Leaders must listen more than talking at this point (do not talk more than a third of the time; ask probing questions). Ask for clarification and determine the root cause of the problem. The OREO technique starts with and ends with thanks/encouragement. Begin the conversation by thanking them for what they have done in the past to help the organization. Next, discuss and resolve the problem/event that occurred. End the conversation with thanks and encouragement for continued great work. Many times I have found that when I looked at an event honestly, I played a role in not getting the employee ready – it is often a training issue. We can work that issue together.

---

TP: If you talk more than a third of the time in counseling sessions, you won't get the best information needed to resolve the issue. The employee should do most of the talking because they know first-hand details of what caused the problem.

---

Be sure to show the people how their performance impacts the success of the organization using measures/metrics. This will allow them to fully understand why they (measures) are important and how their improvements equate to organizational improvements. The metrics should be in a format where they can see them continually and with opportunities for suggesting improvements and innovation.

Finally, as I conclude this chapter on developing others, I want to discuss a very important topic – mentors. If you do not have mentors (notice it is plural meaning more than one is critical for success) for your life, work, family, or financial, you may not be accomplishing all you can. Mentors are critical to your organizational and personal achievement. However, you must never be mentored by someone who is not being mentored. Your mentors need to be constantly improving just like they ask you to do. I truly believe that people are either getting smarter or dumber. With your permission, mentors help you negotiate life and help you get smarter in a deliberate manner. Mentors share insights and experiences to help shelter you from doing the same dumb things they have previously done.

**TP: Mentors can help shelter and protect you from lessons they have learned personally or from the faults of others around them. They can substantially improve your organizational and personal life by sharing those lessons.**

Mentoring can either be done informally or formally. Informal mentoring is just that – moments in time where I ask someone else questions. This can last a short period of time or a couple of years. There is no agreement about a plan. There is no accountability. Formal mentoring requires regular meetings to determine if the mentee is moving with purpose toward their plan which is developed. The mentee allows the mentor to hold them accountable for their (mentee) own dreams and the pursuit of those dreams.

**TP: You really need to actively solicit mentors for your life and work.**

I truly enjoy the formal mentoring. I have 10 challenges my formal mentees must do. They must:

1. Love life and live it passionately. I simply cannot stand whining crybabies who want to blame others rather than work on improving their life.

2. Dream big with courageous goals. If the dream for your life is something you can do by yourself – the dream is too small. A big dream requires mentors and friends to help you achieve it.

3. Take care of your health. Only you can be responsible for your health. If you lose your health, your dreams may go as well.

4. Nourish your mind and spirit by reading/thinking. You must devote some time to reading leadership books IF you are going to get better and to see things differently. You must also get around people who see the world differently than you.

5. Expect the best from people and life. People can be messy in their lives but try to see the best in them.

6. Find something to love in every person. This thought connects to number 5 but adds the necessity to see the value in everyone's unique contribution.

7. Associate with well-wishers. Get around positive people who see life for what it is – an adventure to the very end.

8. Have a sense of wonder. Be amazed every day! We should all regress periodically and see life with a sense of what could be and not as what will never be.

9. Learn to say "NO" periodically. We must tell people "NO" if it does not agree with your plan of development. I am not suggesting telling our boss "NO" but sometimes others can distract us from focusing on our goals.

10. Write down your goals. YOU must write down your goals on paper and review them periodically – with a formal/informal mentor

if possible. You must have your personal life plan congruent with your organizational plan.

---

TP: Your personal strategic plan (PSP) and your organization's strategic plan (OSP) need to work together for you to really feel as though you are making a difference.

---

# CHAPTER 7
# QUESTIONS AND ANSWERS

**Question: What should I do if I don't have an IDP/PDP?**

You will have to process the requirement on your own if your organization does not have these. I suggest you use the following format initially and expand as needed. The following thoughts/questions should focus your time and action at work.

My strengths (3) _____

My weaknesses (3) _____

My opportunities (3) _____

My threats/challenges (3) _____

(normally time, money, and family support)

My most important job at work (3) _____
_____

What does it take to move up at my work (3) _____
_____

What skills/knowledge do I need to move up (3) _____
_____

Question: How can I avoid "getting dumber"?

The three most important ways are:

1. mentor suggestions on how to improve,

2. reading books and doing book reports (with groups or on your own), and,

3. being systematic about what skills and knowledge you need for your future goals. Do not believe that your education will sustain you over the long haul of your work life.

Do not believe that the college education/degree or high school diploma you received many years ago will sustain you over the long haul of your work life.

Question: What should I do if an employee thinks they know my job requirements but really do not?

It boils down to communication. If it is an employee, suggest you both share the top three job/tasks that have to get done in a day. Ask questions of each other concerning comments about those jobs to dig a little deeper. If your employee thinks you are not doing the right job, consider taking them to a higher level meeting and having them observe the higher level requirements that they may have never imagined before.

Question: What is the best way to empower my staff?

A three step approach. First, make sure they understand their job. This may require you sitting with them or having the best trainer in the office sit with them and make sure they can do the job/task assigned. Second, have them teach you how to do it. Teaching will cause them to really burn the lessons into their processes for completing work. Lastly, monitor their performance and make sure they are being successful by showing how their measures/performance fits with the organization as a whole. Share the measures with them and your measures as well so they can see the big picture.

**Question: How do I find a good mentor?**

There are mentors at work who are doing a great job and they are known for good work. Mentors are encouraging and inspiring people who you look up to as successful. A good mentor cares about your success and freely shares sound advice based upon their experiences – good and bad. Mentors need to be cultivated to help you negotiate life and work. Once you believe you have found a mentor, inquire about how they may be able to help you. Caution: You have to be honest in this endeavor and make sure the person you are talking to will not use your candidness and honesty against you.

Some of your best mentors may be outside of the work environment. They can be very candid with you because they are not involved in the day-to-day activities nor do they care about what others think at the workplace.

It is not a good practice to only have mentors within your organization. You have to expand your network to find mentors away from work. Never only have work mentors – never. Take a look at the chart below about how to find mentors outside of work.

Family members may be a great source for mentors. If they are still active in the workforce.

 Friends can also be a source for mentors providing they will tell you the truth in order to help you grow.

 Other people you know or people your friends know may be a source of mentors.

 People who know people who know you. These acquaintances can be very helpful. The people you know are also known as connectors.

 A religious institution is the best place to find mentors who will really care deeply about your development.
Other groups such as social clubs could also be a great source.

# CHAPTER 8 – INSIST ON EXCELLENCE AND MEASURES.

## HAVE INDIVIDUAL AND ORGANIZATIONAL SUCCESS DETERMINED BY WELL-DEFINED GOALS.

---

Ongoing, continuous, non-stop personal development literally assures you that there is no limit to what you can accomplish.  —*Brian Tracy*

The noblest search is the search for excellence.  —*Lyndon B. Johnson*

We are what we repeatedly do. Excellence, then, is not an act, but a habit. —*Aristotle*

Be a yardstick of quality. Some people aren't used to an environment where excellence is expected.  —*Steve Jobs*

Desire is the key to motivation, but it's determination and commitment to an unrelenting pursuit of your goal - a commitment to excellence - that will enable you to attain the success you seek.  —*Mario Andretti*


We must, as Leaders, insist on excellence. Initially, Leaders need to take some time to identify and measure those goals that are critical to success and excellence. This is an obvious conversation with your boss to determine those crucial goals that will lead to organizational and personal success.

---

**TP: Talk with your supervisor to identify the three most critical and essential tasks that you need to accomplish to help the organization meet or exceed its vision, mission, and values (strategic plan). Write them down and stay focused on them.**

---

As an example, one of my leadership jobs was to operate a warehouse. We had to ship and receive supplies as well as take care of walk-in customers. I came up with three goals and placed those on each employee's Individual Development Plan (IDP) or Personal Development Plan (PDP). The goals were Customer Service/Satisfaction, Employment Development, and Resource Management (financial management). Each employee had to tell me what they were doing to address those goals when I would walk around the office and warehouse area (Roundings).

---

**TP: You need to develop three work-related goals and the associated measures in agreement with your supervisor. This will make sure your work counts toward the bigger picture and what the supervisor deems important. As difficult as it may seem, you need to work on what the supervisor wants to accomplish.**

---

After you have the three or so goals (never more than seven), you and your supervisor need to develop ways to accurately measure those goals. The measurements need to be placed visually around the office in some manner so everyone – and I do mean everyone – can view the goals and the organizational progress. These charts need to be updated when the figures change so the most up to date data is available. The period of time for updating depends upon the type of goal and the frequency of change. As an example, if the measures applicable to the goal only change monthly, that would be the frequency. If the measures only change semi-annually, that would be the frequency.

As an example, my good friend Terry May, who is the CEO of Mesa Products (Malcolm Baldrige Award Winner; Best in US Award), has a large chart that he addresses each Monday with all of his employees to let them know exactly where the organization is and the success or failure of their work. The work measures with total transparency are linked to possible bonuses and awards. There are no secrets, the measures must be moving up (up is good).

---

**TP: Measures (supporting data/results) should be available for all employees all the time. This may be limited sometimes based upon proprietary data.**

---

There are a number of goal-setting attributes, which have been the subject of extensive research (Encyclopedia of Business, n.d.). There are four distinct attributes which are specificity, difficulty, acceptance, and commitment which will be discussed in some detail below.

1) Specificity – Research, from a number of scholars, indicates a direct connection between goal specificity and employee performance; the more specific the goal, the higher the performance. Goals need to be very specific for achievement for each employee, each section, each group, and the organization as a whole. The goals must come from the organizational strategic plan and be congruent with the vision, mission, and values.

2) Difficulty - Difficulty must be a consideration in determining goals. If goals are too easy, it does not require innovation and positive risk taking to achieve them. If they are too hard, the organization will feel defeated before it begins to achieve them. Organizational goals should be difficult

and require maximum effort. Do not get this maximum effort confused with working more hours but working on the right priorities. People will fill their day; make sure it is on the right priorities. I had a CEO tell me once they have had goals for seven years and never missed one goal in any department. More than likely the organizational goals are too easy!

3) Acceptance - Acceptance of the goals by the employees is critical. They must own the goals and look forward to their completion. If the Leader can tie in incentives of some kind, that would be a plus. Barring incentives, the Leader needs to find an enemy, something to fight, in order to make the goals realistic. Each employee should accept their goals in order to make the organization better and fulfill their intrinsic definition of success.

4) Commitment - My grandmother once said to me "Commitment means giving up your right to have an excuse" (Grandma McGuire, 1960). Therefore I truly believe employees need a commitment toward the goals. The Leader must ensure they do not allow excuses. A very few of my students in my MBA classes make excuses for being unable to complete assignments. Sometimes the excuses are valid and sometimes they are not but I still hold them accountable. If I totally let them off from the written requirement, they will try to use an excuse again. More importantly, if they are not held accountable for completing the assignment in some way, the value of the task is diminished. Leaders must demand commitment and not allow weak excuses for not completing priority work. Completing priority work is the key to commitment.

---

TP: The goals align with the vision, mission, and values (strategic plan). They must be specific, difficult (not impossible), requiring acceptance, and commitment. Goals must lead your organization to the next level of achievement.

---

The goals must have a periodic review – quarterly at a minimum. The review must validate if the organizational direction is positive or if we are not making our goals (Armstrong, 2006). Why? Is it personnel issues (capability/capacity)? Mission? Resources? You need to review and see why we are not being successful. You must monitor your success, employee success, and organizational success and all need to be aligned and linked for maximum success.

---

TP: All goals must undergo periodic review and validation. Goals need to be presented by those who are in charge of their monitoring and completion. Everyone must share in accountability.

---

Leaders need to calibrate time, authority, personal involvement, and performance standards while insisting on excellence. Be careful that apathy and complacency do not creep into your organization and excuses are allowed. This apathy/complacency will drag the organization into a tragic downward spiral which could be harder to turn around. Do not let your employees talk you into minor improvements. As an example, I talked to one organization who told me they had met all their goals for five consecutive years. This is a red flag for organizational excellence. I told them the goals were probably too low. If you can meet all of your goals every year, then the organization is not being pushed to achieve excellence. It is strange how some bosses cannot understand that concept, but I must admit it is a hard concept to understand.

---

TP: Remember this – IF you always meet all of the goals assigned each year, then the goals may be too low. The right goals are in place if you meet some goals and consistently make progress on the others.

# CHAPTER 8
# QUESTIONS AND ANSWERS

**Question: What if your organization does not have a strategic plan?**

This is a very good question as a number of organizations where I have worked do not have a formal strategic plan. This will require you at your level to come up with three or four goals based upon your perception of where the organization needs to go. In essence, you will make a small strategic plan for your group. Include measures for each of the goals. Take a look statistically (chart or graph) at your current position and decide on how much you can improve. Take this to your supervisor and have a conversation about it. If they approve your goals, you are on your way to prioritization and measuring of work. If they disapprove, work with them on modifying the list of goals and measures. If they never agree to any goals, don't give up. Work on your own to make both the organization and yourself better. This is your only option without higher supervisor support and agreement.

**Question: What can I do as a Leader if the goals we have are not very specific?**

As with the previous question above, work with your supervisor to establish some specificity for the goals you now have and see if that works. Make sure all employees understand the reason for these specific goals is to help improve organizational performance.

Question: When do goals and their progress need to be reviewed?

Goals need to be reviewed when there is some measure that could help us adjust our work to improve our success in achieving the goals and their measures of success. As an example, if the goals are moving daily with updated data, you may want to evaluate the status on a weekly basis. If the goals do not change (based upon updated data) but once a month, review the goals monthly. If you are in a K-12 setting and you have six-week grading periods, review the status of academic goals at the end of each six weeks. The rule of thumb is that when data is updated, reviews need to occur to make the adjustments necessary to improve performance.

# CHAPTER 9 – PRAISE.

"Everyone has an invisible sign hanging from their neck saying, 'Make me feel important.' Never forget this message when working with people." —*Mary Kay Ash*

"I can live for two months on a good compliment." —*Mark Twain*

"I have yet to find the man, however exalted his station, who did not do better work and put forth greater effort under a spirit of approval than under a spirit of criticism." —*Charles M. Schwab*

"Leaders should be into the praising business. Targeted, warranted praise is a very important motivator and sustainability issue for any organization. Use this motivational tool wisely." —*C. U. (Mac) McGuire III*

Praise is essential to well-being in almost any environment. Praise of work done well leads to more work done well. Praise can work to encourage, energize, and motivate all types of workers from all generations. Therefore, the targeted and warranted use of praise can be a force multiplier and lead to more successful individuals.

I once happened upon a first grade class headed to the lunch room. The teacher stopped the mob of youngsters weaving down the hall in random order at the door of the cafeteria. She asked them to line up and some did and some didn't. She then began to call them by name and each one lined up – they wanted to hear their name in association with something good. I think most adults (the people who work for you) want the same thing – to have their name called out and it be associated with something good.

In my humble opinion, there are seven considerations when praising employees:

1) <u>Be specific and factual.</u> You need to be specific about what you are praising. Let the employee know, beyond any shadow of a doubt, what they did to warrant the praise. Make sure you know what they did! It is important to be specific about what event you are praising because it has been my experience that if you give praise for a specific behavior, that behavior will most likely continue – so be careful how and when you praise. If the behavior is not what you want to see (praising for inadequate work) – you could get more of that.

2) <u>Treat each employee differently.</u> When you praise an extrovert, they like it loud with plenty of words. If you are praising an introvert, they may want it to be accomplished between you and them in a quiet place. In other words, praise your employees in the manner that is most effective for their personality. This may take some time, but as you begin to know your employees, you will know what motivates them to do even better work as well as improve morale. You may make some mistakes at first, but keep praising and you will improve morale. Above all, treat each individual who works for you with dignity and respect.

3) <u>Be positive and look for good behavior/actions.</u> You need to search out the positive accomplishments of your people. Look for success and praise them quickly. Do not wait! Give flowers to the living! Many, many organizations wait for employees to retire to tell them how much they WERE appreciated. Some organizations even have policies about the awards employees receive upon retirement that are usually the same whether the

employees were outstanding or were just average. Don't wait for retirement to tell an employee how great they are and the value they added to the organization. Tell them now and watch how they can positively affect others.

4) Establish a Praise Culture. Encourage employees to praise each other. Supervisors are not the only ones who can praise people for their unique contribution. You can praise your peers, your subordinates, and yes, even your supervisors when these individuals do something to help the organization. Recognizing the contributions of individuals, whoever they are, creates a positive environment. People blossom better in that environment. Success breeds success!

5) Praise publicly. I know this may shock some of you who are introverts, but we need to praise publicly so that other employees see what good looks like. We need to be vocal with our praise. I know some don't like to be placed in the spotlight but let me assure you that the organization needs public praise to set the course.

6) Measures can help decide when to praise. Individual and organizational goals that are achieved provide Leaders with a grand opportunity to praise their employees. When individuals or groups accomplish difficult goals or receive positive customer compliments, Leaders should use targeted praise effectively. Leaders need to be careful in praising groups. Did everyone participate? Did everyone contribute? Unmerited praise may not achieve much goodwill and may hurt the organizational effort to improve performance for all.

7) Start a praise wall. In the military, we placed specific storyboards on the wall documenting how a group of individuals and supervisors made a significant difference in a project or process improvement. We outlined the steps taken, the problem solving approach utilized, and the money saved or cost avoidance achieved. This was instrumental in other significant improvements as others wanted their name and pictures on the wall. It really works!

---

TP: Be intentional about your role in encouraging employees. Watch for what it does to move your organization forward.

---

Remember to use praise as a Leadership tool to highlight the achievement of individuals and segments (parts of the organizational chart) of the organization. If done well, specific and targeted praise accelerates the positive environment that all Leaders are looking for in the organization. One warning when praising, this is not a time to give a lecture or discuss bad things. Just bask in the positive moment.

# CHAPTER 9
# QUESTIONS AND ANSWERS

**Question: What are examples of good praise?**

Praise can be as simple as passing by someone's desk or cubicle and telling them how much you appreciated their efforts on a project. It could be as much as getting the person a raise, stipend, or recognition from the next level supervisor. Praise comes in all types of events. Awards dinners/staff meetings are examples where you take time to recognize people for measured success such as a 10% increase in customer satisfaction in the last six months. I hope you get the idea.

**Question: How do you ensure that you recognize more than a few select employees?**

This will almost always be a problem to resolve. Some of your employees will have great success. Their personality, their expertise, their drive and ambition, and work ethic will place them ahead of peers. Your job is to look for those people who can do jobs/tasks well and praise them. As an example, some workers will be slower in finishing jobs/tasks but may do a more thorough job. Look for ways to praise everyone but some may not ever achieve the status you are looking for in work completion. The trick will be to praise them without pandering to them and that is a fine line.

Question: How does praise really affect the workplace/morale?

As mentioned earlier, praise can be a force multiplier (get more from the same amount of people and resources). Praise can help focus all employees on what the Leader says is important. Most employees want to follow the lead of the Leader, but they need to fully understand what is important. Praising the right work can have a significant impact on morale as employees will know what is important and how necessary their contribution is to organizational importance.

# CHAPTER 10 – SET THE RIGHT EXAMPLE.

## (I REALLY HATE THIS ONE!)

---

"Example is not the main thing in influencing others, it is the only thing! Example is leadership." —*Albert Schweitzer*

"Few things are harder to put up with than the annoyance of a good example." —*Mark Twain*

"Go before the people with your example, and be laborious in their affairs." —*Confucius*

"A good example is far better than a good precept." —*Dwight L. Moody*

I hate this chapter because it is very difficult to accomplish. I have tried so hard here, but I often rate myself as woefully inadequate. Setting the right example can be extremely difficult and will cause you pain if you are serious about it. However, Leaders must have the ability to self-evaluate and determine where shortcomings exist to ensure you walk your talk.

When I became a company commander, I followed the Seven Values of the United States Army. Those time tested values are loyalty, duty, respect, selfless service, honor, integrity, and personal courage (http://www.army. mil/values/index.html). It is critically important to follow the values of the organization in which you serve or to follow time-tested examples of values such as with the Bible. Values are the true essence of your being and what you stand for.

One day in formation with my soldiers, I announced the requirement for all of us to follow these Seven Army Values and to the need to help each other follow them. I went on to say that if anyone saw me not following a value, they were to inform me immediately, regardless of rank or status. My experienced First Sergeant, Joe Gartman, cautioned me about making a big issue of the values because there is so much left to a verbal translation of what the values stand for. I chose not listen to his wise counsel. I chose poorly.

After three days, I told them to stop informing me. While I knew that I had not violated any of the values, it looked like I did from their perspective. I realized each soldier had a different definition for each of the values. I therefore had to communicate and discuss the true definition of each value what they meant in the daily workplace.

Make sure you know the organizational values and have them defined in writing. This can help to eliminate or reduce confusion especially when the definitions of those organizational values collide with your own. Make sure you discuss the values with all concerned and explain theory (what they truly mean) and application (how it looks in our daily work).

---

TP: Make sure your people understand the definitions of the values clearly so as not to be confused when the terms are used. Communicate the values well – personal and organizational.

---

I recommend here you take some time and evaluate yourself (self-evaluation) with a list of your personal strengths, weaknesses, opportunities, and threats (SWOT). The SWOT will enable you to initially assess yourself and determine where you may have shortcomings. Your friends and family along with mentors that have known you for a while may be a great resource to help you the first time you complete your SWOT. Remember to be honest with yourself and suggest others participating understand the SWOT is designed to help you. If your friends, family, and mentors are not honest with you about your SWOT, your assessment will not be successful.

First, let's look at a personal Life SWOT. This is how you are all the time. We will take a look at the Work SWOT later. I recommend you limit the number of strengths, weaknesses, opportunities, and threats to three so you can focus. I am sharing my personal Life SWOT to use as a model as you begin to work on yours.

In my personal Life SWOT, I realize and have been told by others that my love for people shows quickly, that I am a good teacher, and that I have the innate ability to make things simple (although my wife may disagree as she helped to edit this book). My weaknesses include loving people (sometimes our strengths are also our weaknesses if we do it too much), talking too fast when excited, and making things too simple sometimes. My opportunities include growing people (mentoring), being a better communicator to help others grow, and improving my education (I truly love school and school work). My threats include time to do what I want to do, money to sustain my family, and family support so I can consult, teach and write.

| Strengths | Weaknesses | Opportunities | Threats |
|---|---|---|---|
| 1) Love People; All People | Love People; People take advantage of my helpful attitude | Grow People; Mentor others to achieve their life/work goals | Time; I must be very good at time management |
| 2) Good Teacher; Have the ability to transmit messages | Talk too fast when I teach | Be a better Communicator; Be able to state messages in a number of different venues | Money; Realize I cannot help everyone I would like to help |
| 3) Make things simple; Work diligently to make things understood by others | May try to make life/ work too simple sometimes | Continue to improve education; Improve MBA classes at UMHB and community classes at UT Austin | Family Support; Need support to work with others |

*Mac McGuire's Personal Life SWOT*

Now use this chart to write your personal Life SWOT. Remember this is your personal Life SWOT so to speak and how you see yourself all the time. Remember to engage those people in your life that will tell you the truth. If they don't tell the truth, you may miss some key components of your SWOT that could help you reach your personal goals. Your Life SWOT may be similar to mine where your strength is also a weakness or they may be totally unrelated.

| Strengths | Weaknesses | Opportunities | Threats |
|-----------|------------|---------------|---------|
| 1 | | | |
| 2 | | | |
| 3 | | | |

The organizational Work SWOT for you should also be completed. The organizational Work SWOT may be a little different from your Life SWOT or it may be similar. Are there disconnects with your personal SWOT and your organizational SWOT? Again, I give you an example of my organizational SWOT from my McGuire & Associates Consulting business (www.macmcguire.com).

| Strengths | Weaknesses | Opportunities | Threats |
|---|---|---|---|
| Quality Leadership Training; Leadership Development Programs | May be too blunt sometimes; People may need to be validated first; Lack patience for people who do not try or give excuses for working hard | Tell the truth but tone down my presentation as to not sound threatening | Some people and organizations do not want the truth; I need to get away from those because I will never be truly appreciated for my efforts |
| Good Author; I love to write | Want to be a Great author; Admired by others for that particular talent | Write more; Focus on writing improvement | Can I show continual improvement in my writing; How can I measure that improvement? |
| Good Professor; My evaluations indicate I am good | Good Professor; My evaluations indicate I am good but I seek greatness | Continue to work hard on my classes both at UT Austin and UMHB Belton | Having the time to fully develop new material; Reading five books a month minimum |

*Mac McGuire Work Life SWOT (McGuire & Associates Consulting)*

Your organizational Work SWOT deals specifically with your work life. It is similar to the Personal Life SWOT in completion. Here we may need to get a supervisor, some peers, and maybe some trusted subordinates to help us. Use the chart below to write in your information.

| Strengths | Weaknesses | Opportunities | Threats |
|---|---|---|---|
|  |  |  |  |
|  |  |  |  |
|  |  |  |  |

TP: There is a need for you to assess your SWOT in Life and at Work. Are there problems where your personal Life SWOT and the Work SWOT are in conflict? Are you getting better at work and in life? Or, are you getting worse? Have you stopped growing? Self-evaluate your personal life and yourself at the workplace, see where you are and aren't, and be prepared to take some action to improve your situation.

Now that we have completed our Life and Work SWOT's, are they aligned or disconnected and do we know it? As an example, are your strengths connected to your opportunities or not? Are you working in a field that is suited to your talents? Are you doing work you truly enjoy?

The final question is a tough one. Are you a prisoner or a volunteer? If you find that you are a prisoner, it may be time to expand your networks and look to move to another job. If you are a volunteer, there is a good chance you are in the right place. It is up to you.

After you have completed your personal life and organizational SWOT, it is time for you to grow. I have included a step-by-step instrument to put everything in a neat process that you can systematically evaluate and move forward. The following diagram may help provide you with certain steps ensuring a systematic process. I will explain each step so you can truly understand when it is time to move on to the next step.

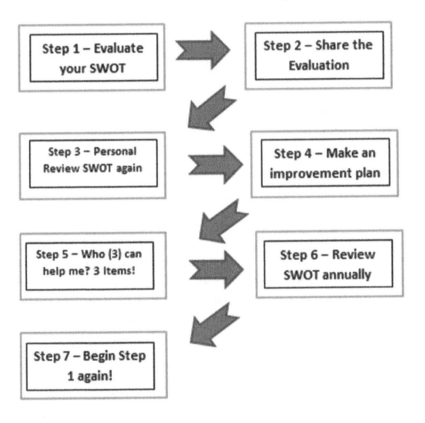

*SWOT Evaluation Instrument (McGuire, 2012)*

Step 1 involves your evaluation of your SWOT. I recommend you do this evaluation with at least three people who know you in your personal life and three who know you at work. You will need to give the evaluators of your SWOT permission to be very honest and candid for the purpose of helping you grow and be a better person. I strongly believe, we are either getting better as a person (more experienced; wiser; more knowledgeable) or getting worse (failing to seize opportunities; in a rut; trapped in the past). Which is it for you and your growth?

---

TP: You have to select people and give them permission to be honest with you in determining your SWOT. Close friends who agree with you on everything you discuss are probably not the right choice.

---

Step 2 requires a sharing of the evaluation with the six people (minimum) and determining if it is accurate from their perspective. Remember that the people you select (from Step 1) must be able to tell you the truth – good and bad. Remember we all have both and it is okay. The point is to continue to improve. If you enlist a friend who tells you that you do not have weaknesses, then you need to find someone else to help you. Let me also warn you here that you need to evaluate what they say and determine if there is merit in their comments. Do not discount their input without consideration.

---

TP: After you have completed the evaluation with input from the six people, go back to them with your completed list of strengths, weaknesses, opportunities, and threats, validating each comment and asking for clarity. You must make sure you fully understand their comments.

---

Step 3 mandates your personal review of the SWOT after getting input from the six people. What trends have developed? What changes need to be made? Does your attitude play a role in a positive or negative way?

**TP: Take a good hard look at who you are and what you represent by your SWOT.**

Step 4 recommends an improvement plan. You must develop an improvement plan based upon what you have encountered with the evaluators (six people). What is your SWOT showing after the evaluation? This is where you can work with a mentor to outline how to use your strengths and how to work on weaknesses. If you have a weakness that is hard to overcome, in your opinion, find ways to put yourself in situations (Life/Work) that maximizes your strengths.

**TP: The improvement plan needs to address your SWOT in total (Life and Work). Who are you really? What do other people see in you most often?**

Step 5 requires finding three people to help you with your Life and Work situations. These are people who you see as successful and would make good role models. These people (mentors), when chosen correctly, can really help you grow and grow faster than you could on your own (for more on mentoring, see Chapter 7).

**TP: Identify who can help you get better in the foreseeable future. Try to spend quality time with them and allow them to help you in becoming better.**

Step 6 is the annual review of your SWOT. There needs to be an annual review to determine if you are making progress towards improvement. This annual review needs to be conducted with those individuals selected in Step 5.

TP: Use the three people selected in Step 5 to help you develop a plan for your improvement and allow them to hold you accountable.

Step 7 takes us back to begin Step 1 again. These steps can work to make you a better person IF you will evaluate yourself honestly and procure the appropriate mentors.

TP: Self-evaluation is critical to growing wiser and more knowledgeable about life and work. You must have a willingness to improve in order to make it work.

One day a young wife asked me to meet with her husband because he had trouble keeping a job. I met with the young man and he brought his Work SWOT with him. He had a number of strengths but no weaknesses. When I inquired about a list of his weaknesses, he informed me he had none that he could think of at the time. I asked him who developed his SWOT and he said he did it himself. He had been fired from six jobs in the last nine years. He informed me several people attempted to help him at work but he refused their help. He told me that he was smarter than any boss he had ever had after working about two weeks at each job. That is an example of someone who either does not understand the importance of self-evaluation or he is unable to accept constructive criticism or perhaps both.

We began to talk about what previous supervisors had told him when they fired him and he still could not see any problems. He assured me that he knew his supervisors were the real problem in his work life. As we talked, I realized that he just did not get it. I suggested that he review his Work SWOT with three people and I have not heard from him again. He left dejected and told me that his wife told him I could fix personal problems. I can't help a person who will not listen and believes he is a legend in his own mind. Don't be like that! Realize that we all have strengths, weaknesses, opportunities to improve ourselves, and threats to defeat our achievement and act accordingly.

---

TP: If you can't look objectively at your own SWOT, then you can never move forward and be all you can be. Listen to the wise sayings of others and work constantly and forever to improve.

---

In order to set the right example, I must tell you that you are known by the company you keep. Stay away from the whining crybabies in your personal and organizational life. They will drag you down and keep you from doing two things – 1) seeing life properly and 2) making the most of life. Those whining crybabies are never satisfied and always think someone is out to get them. They work hard on getting out of work rather than working hard.

---

TP: Don't spend much time with people who constantly give excuses and blame others.

---

Along this same line of thinking, be careful who you hire. When selecting personnel to hire, make sure you hire the highest quality and, if possible, hire those who are smarter than you (this has never been a problem for me).

TP: Hire carefully for the character you need to fulfill your mission in the organization. My grandmother used to say that "character is what you are in the dark."

# CHAPTER 10
# QUESTIONS AND ANSWERS

**Question: What if I disagree with the input for my Life or Work SWOT?**

There are possibilities that you will disagree with some of the input on your SWOT. My advice would be to take some time to reflect on your input from others and see if there is a potential to gain from their insight. Remember you gave them the permission to tell you the truth. If they are trying to help you, they are probably not lying. Remember it is their perspective, so listen to them.

**Question: Why is having a SWOT so important?**

A SWOT is a measure of a point in time. We all need to take inventory of our life and try to make continual adjustments for improvements. The SWOT can help you position yourself for the future based upon what you want to do and where you want to go. It could be your roadmap for the future.

**Question: How do I find the right six people to help me evaluate my SWOT?**

Based upon my conversations with students in classes that I teach, this can be challenging. I suggest you talk with personal friends (away from work), your spouse, children, parents, pastors/religious people, and community groups for the Life SWOT. For the Work

SWOT, I suggest friends at work, supervisors, retired people you have worked with in the past, places where you have volunteered, community groups where you have worked, peers, and subordinates. Write all of these potential people down and circle those who you trust to help you.

**Question: How will I know, really know, if I am getting better?**

Let everyone know you are determined to grow and change. Announce it and then you can claim it. Some of the byproducts of growing in a positive way include becoming more respected at home. As you begin to change your view of life and work, people around you will see you struggle with improving. At work, you will encounter more difficult opportunities, challenges with new changes, promotions, and importance in meetings because people will notice a different you. You may be asked to lead work units as more and more people see your dedication and growth. You will be able rely on knowledge learned from your mentors and books you have read. At home, your immediate and extended families may see the change in you as you begin to overcome your weaknesses.

I would be less than honest with you if I told you that your growth is dependent on only you. If you think you can be all you can be on your own, you are missing the experience and wisdom of others who can accelerate your growth. Opportunities have to be sought after and <u>you will have to step up</u> to take on more complex tasks at home and at work.

# CHAPTER 11 – EMPOWER YOUR PEOPLE.

"Authentic empowerment is the knowing that you are on purpose, doing God's work, peacefully and harmoniously." —*Wayne Dyer*

"There's a basic philosophy here that by empowering...workers you'll make their jobs far more interesting, and they'll be able to work at a higher level than they would have without all that information just a few clicks away." —*Bill Gates*

"Few things help an individual more than to place responsibility upon him, and to let him know you trust him." —*Booker T. Washington*

Empowerment appears to be clearly misunderstood by most organizations based upon my experience. Additionally, in the books I have read, there are a number of definitions suggesting misunderstandings regarding empowerment and how Leaders can accomplish empowerment.

In my humble opinion, based upon my research and experiences, empowerment involves selecting of the right people for the job, teaching problem solving skills, giving them dedicated training about the job, and development of a trusting relationship.

Selection involves making sure the individual has the capability and capacity to do the job correctly. This can involve mental, physical, or socio-emotional capability/capacity. Do they have that? Are you setting them up for success or failure?

If the answer is yes regarding the employee capability and capacity, then did you provide the right job training? Have you actually shown them how to do the job and seen the employee have success? All too often training is not done well. You must teach your people how to solve problems on a day-to-day basis.

Lastly, do you trust them to do the job right after you have shown them how to do it? Do you reinforce good work by praising them? If you have selected the right person, trained them and taught them problem solving, then you must trust they can do the job unless monitoring proves otherwise.

---

TP: Empowerment involves selection of the right people, problem solving, job training, and developing trusting relationships.

---

Selection of the right people involves knowing the capability and capacity of your people. Are you asking them to do a job that does not fit their skills and knowledge? Be deliberate in this evaluation of your people.

Leaders need to seek input from subordinates when and where possible. Leaders must encourage employees to be honest in discussions about problems and potential solutions. Most of all employees must be honest. Now I must touch on a difficult subject in connection with seeking input from employees – sometimes you need to give your staff permission to respectfully disagree with you. There is an old East Texas saying, "A little friction is needed for traction." If your people always agree with you, then someone is not telling the truth. Leaders have to cognitively understand that they do not and cannot have the right answers all the time; that is impossible even for the best Leaders. Allow your employees the freedom to discuss problems honestly thereby enabling the Leader to get all the information needed to make the best decision on behalf of the organization.

---

TP: Leaders should not cultivate/hire "Yes" people. True Leaders should need/want/desire honest feedback/discussions/criticism directed toward organizational improvements with solid, well thought out ideas. Without honesty, Leaders may miss out on critical information needed to make the best decisions that will help the organization be successful and meet the Vision, Mission and Goals.

---

Problem solving training needs its own area in this book. Teaching employees how to solve problems extends the basic training given to them about the job.

In addressing problems, I have found asking four or five "why" questions can most often lead to the root cause of the problem. Often a symptom is identified rather than the actual problem. It works like this. In one of my consulting opportunities with a for-profit organization, I had a Human Resource Leader tell me that the biggest problem the organization was facing was that they were "hiring dumb people." Let's take a look at that initial problem and evaluate it.

| Problem | Why Question |
|---|---|
| Initial Statement of the Problem<br>We are hiring dumb people | First "Why" Question.<br>Why are you hiring dumb people? |
| Response 1.<br>That is the only type of person applying for our jobs. | Second "Why" Question.<br>Why do you think only dumb people are applying for your jobs? |
| Response 2.<br>Well we are not taking enough time to really screen people. | Third "Why" Question.<br>Why are you not taking sufficient time to hire the right person? |
| Response 3.<br>Our company policies dictate an expedited procedure when we have strict timelines for product delivery. | Fourth "Why" Question.<br>Why does the company have an expedited procedure? |
| Response 4.<br>Our expedited procedure is used for critical hiring situations. | Fifth "Why" Question.<br>Why is the expedited hiring procedure being used exclusively rather than taking time to hire the right person? |

| Response 5. | Root Cause of Initial Statement of the |
|---|---|
| Our expedited hiring proce-dure is easier to use and takes less time for our supervisors. It was designed for emergency use only. | Problem. The expedited procedure was designed for emergency situations but is being used now for all situations. |

*Five Why Questions Example for Determining the Root Cause of a Problem.*

Now let's take a look at the same Five Why Questions in an educational setting. In talking with a principal at a school, the problem stated was that the middle school had the highest eighth-grade drop-out rate in the district.

| | |
|---|---|
| Initial Statement of the Problem. Our middle school has the highest eighth-grade drop-out rate in the district | First "Why" Question. Why do you have the highest drop-out rate of eighth graders? |
| Response 1. Some kids are not trying. | Second Why Question. Why do you say that? |
| Response 2. Some kids just will not do their homework. | Third "Why" Question. Why do you think they are not do-ing their homework? |
| Response 3. They just don't care and the parents must not care either. | Fourth "Why" Question. Why do you think the kids and the parents do not care? |
| Response 4. They do not see education as a priority. | Fifth Why Question. Why do they not see education as a priority? |
| Response 5. Perhaps educators have not taken enough time to impress the necessity on the parents and kids. | Root Cause of Initial Statement of the Problem. It may be that the educators need to work more closely with parents and children and impress upon then the relevance and necessity of education. |

This discussion can be included in Health Care organizations as well but I think you get the point. Routinely, it has been my experience, and there is some research to back this statement, that Leaders can best solve problems by asking questions to identify the root cause. If Leaders do not address the root cause, the real problem will never go away.

Whenever possible, data should be used to address problems. One caveat, data can be manipulated by the humans inputting the source information. But I would be remiss if I did not mention the need to collect data regarding problems to ensure you work on the root cause.

---

TP: Leaders must find root causes to problems to make sure they are solved. Collection and review of data is an essential element in problem solving.

---

Leaders must empower their staff by teaching them multiple approaches for problem solving. One of the best techniques for problem solving is to teach and use Bloom's Taxonomy. While this is most often associated with education and higher learning, the Taxonomy can also be applied effectively in all types of settings where gathering and evaluation of data is used to resolve problems. The next chart has the original version of the Taxonomy from a 1956 study by Benjamin Bloom. On the right is an updated study completed in the 1990s by Lorin Anderson (former Bloom student) which has been adapted for the 21st century captured in a book by Pohl (2000). Both Bloom's and Pohl's versions have applications for empowerment. Leaders need to teach employees how to do research to solve organizational problems by the systematic evaluation of the data and analysis of the past, current, and future state.

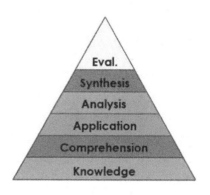 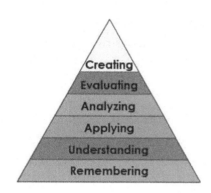

*Bloom's Taxonomy (1956)*                          *Pohl (2000)*

| Bloom's Taxonomy (1956) | Pohl's revision (1990s) | McGuire adaptation (2012); Application for an organization or in your personal life |
|---|---|---|
| Knowledge (lowest) | Remembering | What can the past tell us? What does our data show? How do we define our past? |
| Comprehension | Understanding | Where are we now? How do we really know? |
| Application | Applying | Where do we need to go? |
| Analysis | Analyzing | What does the micro and macro analysis show? Are you sure? |
| Synthesis | Evaluating | Where do we need to go? How can we best integrate improvements? |
| Evaluation (highest) | Creating | Did we learn some new knowledge or information? What new policies need to come forth? New and updated processes? |

*Bloom's Taxonomy, Pohl's Revisions, and McGuire (2013) Adaptations*

---

TP: Leaders need to be able and willing to ask questions to solve problems and realize the first response to stating a problem is not the real problem.

---

Job training is required to set all employees up for success. Success breeds success and failure breeds failure. What are you breeding in your organization? Make sure you have effective and timely training opportunities for all of your employees. As jobs are encountered, Leaders need to assess if the people have been sufficiently trained. Some training can come from inside, but some may be needed from outside the organization. Some employees, because of job complexity or volume, may require more training, but make sure everyone has the opportunity to grow both personally and organizationally. If the employee is deliberately developed to meet the needs of the organization, they can be better prepared for job completion and innovation (faster, smarter, and cheaper).

Training assessments should come from the analysis of the organizational vision/mission/values and from the first level supervisor. The need for supervisory and teambuilding training should be consolidated with the Human Resource (HR) Department in most cases. As an example, if the first level Leaders suggests teambuilding training to improve the organization, the request for that training should be submitted to the HR department for consolidation. HR should determine how widespread the need exists for teambuilding training based upon all supervisors input to be systematic throughout the organization. Classes should then be developed in-house (if the expertise is available) or contracted with an external source and offered to all departments to ensure all needs are addressed.

---

TP: Effective Leaders ensure employees are set up for success and not failure by deliberate and intentional training centered on helping employees grow to substantially improve organizational measures.

---

Finally, after the employees have been empowered through selection, job training, and problem solving, Leaders must work on establishing subordinate accountability in order to discipline (Note – Discipline is a Latin word that means to teach) their employees. Leaders must also have appropriate goals achieved on behalf of the organization. I recommend the following considerations:

1) Teach them what right looks like. YOU must show them what the end product of their work should look like and what you want for an output. Sometimes we need to take them through it first. Some would say it is easier to do it myself (like I used to say) but then you will have to do it forever. You would develop and your employees would not develop.

2) Delineate roles. Make sure, without question or mental reservation that you have made their role very clear. Encourage feedback to make sure.

3) Set guidelines. Let them know where they can go and what they can do to accomplish the work. Don't be surprised what action they will take if you fail to make this clear.

4) Trust and believe in them. We must trust our subordinates to do what is right, but first we must set the example and build the relationship.

5) Institute a progressive disciplinary program. Leaders determine the root cause for non-compliance of tasks assigned. 6) Is it can't do or won't do? If the employee failure is can't do; then more extensive training may be needed. If it is found they won't do the job and you need it done, then termination is just around the corner.

6) Promote good work. Leaders praise good work and reward great work. What you praise is what you will get more of in the future.

7) Do not accept incompetency. If the person cannot fit into your organization, Leaders terminate them quickly.

TP: Leaders must constantly evaluate their people (capability/capacity) and decide what they can do to improve opportunities for growth. One big question: Do you have the right people in the right position?

# CHAPTER 11
# QUESTIONS AND ANSWERS

**Question: Why do I need to empower the staff? Does it really make a difference?**

The bottom line regarding empowerment is the need for employees to understand the organizational mission (what we are doing; big picture). After that understanding, targeted training needs to be done. This training emphasizes how to do the jobs/tasks that will support mission accomplishment. Only after the mission is understood and the training is complete, can the employees become empowered to do the job in support of the mission.

It can make a significant difference in one very important component regarding work – buy-in leading to employee engagement. Employee engagement is critical to mission accomplishment. Leaders need employees to buy-in to what the organization is doing, how it is being done, and what we can do to improve it (innovation).

**Question: How can I identify the training needed and if it is best practice?**

Training requirements should include a review of the mental, physical, interpersonal, and psychological needs of the job. Leaders must observe what skills and knowledge are necessary in order to do work effectively and efficiently. As an example, the employees may need teambuilding training to improve working together or customer service training if that component is essential to job accomplishment. Leaders need to decide what training is needed and then assess the capabilities and capacities of the people. Any identified shortcomings need to be addressed in a systematic training program.

The last part of the question regarding best practice is difficult. Research will need to be utilized to determine if proposed training is best practice. Beware of books, articles, and other material that is not research based. Additionally, organizations who have won significant awards for effectiveness such as the Malcolm Baldrige Quality Award Criteria for Performance Improvement would be a best practice organization. Most states have a MBQNA CPE list of organizations to review. Studying their training programs would help any organization with ideas of how to address training requirements.

**Question: How do I encourage staff to be honest with me in problem solving without being fearful that they will lose their job for speaking up?**

Great question! Leaders must cultivate an organizational climate that encourages honest, candid comments to questions concerning the organizational mission, jobs/tasks, and possible ideas for innovation. Problems that occur should be discussed with those employees involved in the solution. Failing to allow this involvement and discussion sets your organization up for minimizing effectiveness. Leaders need to truly understand they do not have all the answers and are not always right. Avoid the temptation to shoot from the hip without allowing employee input.

Question: What data is needed in systematic problem solving?

The data requirement is different for each situation and each problem. Leaders will refer back to the strategic planning document about the vision, mission, and goals to determine what data is needed. There is a direct connection to how you view the problem under the direction outlined by the organizational strategic plan (vision, mission, goals). The data needed should for systematic problem solving should include information helpful to problem resolution.

# CHAPTER 12 – COURAGE.

"Courage is rightly esteemed the first of human qualities . . . because it is the quality which guarantees all others."  —*Winston Churchill*

"One man with courage makes a majority."  —*Andrew Jackson*

"Courage is resistance to fear, mastery of fear - not absence of fear. —*Mark Twain*

"You will never do anything in this world without courage. It is the greatest quality of the mind next to honor."  —*Aristotle*

"Courage is being scared to death—but saddling up anyway." —*John Wayne*

Some of my most notable examples of courage come from George Washington, Branch Rickey, and Rosa Parks. George Washington was known as the "Father of our Country" but is not revered in England's history. He is looked upon as one who swore allegiance to the throne and then ran away from it. He is considered by England as one of the most hated traitors of all time. It took courage knowing if he chose the wrong side and if America did not win its independence, he and perhaps some of his family would surely die a horrible death at the hands of the British. To Americans however, because of his courage to fight for America, he is considered the "Father of our Country."

**TP: Sometimes courage will require going against incredible odds because it is the right thing to do.**

Branch Rickey was the President of the Brooklyn Dodgers. He made the decision to support hiring Jackie Robinson, a "black" baseball player, because he was a good baseball player, but also because he was educated and abstained from alcohol http://www.worldandi.com/newhome/public/2003/march/mtpub.asp. It was 1943 and the Supreme Court had not yet outlawed school segregation. It was five years before President Truman would desegregate the Armed Forces. Branch Rickey, president of the Brooklyn Dodgers began to actively recruit black ballplayers because it was the right thing to do. In 1947, Jackie Robinson, stepped onto the field. It took great courage against incredible odds for both of these men to officially desegregate baseball forever.

**TP: It appears, based in my research for this book and my military experience, that courage may be ill defined for Leaders. Courage could make you very alone and in some very difficult situations, but courage is a vital part of being a Leader and doing what is right when the politics may suggest otherwise. It takes real courage to stand up for what is right.**

Another example deals with Rosa Parks who was a very courageous woman indeed http://www.achievement.org/autodoc/page/par0int-1. She was arrested in 1955 for refusing to give up her seat on the bus when ordered to do so by the bus driver. Her story has been told repeatedly wrong. She was not in the front of the bus where the white people would sit. She sat one row behind the white section. She did take the last seat. After the second or third stop, one white man was left standing. The bus driver told her to let the white man have the seat. She was then arrested for failing to heed the message of the bus driver. She was extraordinarily courageous. Her courage in the face of adversity was incredible because she defied all odds and peacefully fought the system.

---

TP: Even when conventional wisdom says you are wrong, you may be right. Sometimes you may have to take a stand that is not popular with the majority.

---

Now let's discuss your level of courage. I am not sure you will ever face situations like Washington, Rickey, or Parks but you must decide what you will tolerate and where your standards are regarding the difference between right and wrong. Courage may require you to take a stand for your organization, for your people, and maybe, just maybe for your boss. Can you do it or are you willing to do it? Sometimes it means fighting conformity, identifying what is right (the truth), and setting boundaries. In many cases, it will most certainly cause you to be in the minority.

---

TP: You may be required to fight conformity and take the right action, even when your action may not sit well with superiors or your peers. Can you do it? Will you do it? Where is the line for you? You will need to address these questions in your mind prior to having difficult situations thrust on you and then trying to figure it out.

---

Fear is the direct enemy of courage and can defeat you before you even begin to plan. Fear of failure or fear of being on a losing end of a fight figuratively or literally can weaken your spirit and stop you from doing what is right. Mistakes will happen and you will sometimes misjudge situations but let me admonish you to take the high road and do what is right every time. As I am mentoring people of all ages, I am constantly reminded of the fear that lies around most indecision in our lives. The inability to make a decision can lead to a paralysis. Many decisions in my life have been avoided due to fear. Some of my decisions were made in spite of the fear – some were good and some were bad but all had consequences. Do not let fear of the unknown or any other fears limit your decisions and your dream accomplishment.

---

**TP: Fear can immobilize you to inaction rather than action. Overcome your fears or you could be held captive until it is too late to move, or in some cases, forever.**

---

I often get asked this question in my teaching, "How can we know when to show courage?" You need to set standards for yourself and live within the standards established by you and your organization. When others betray those standards of conduct, courage will be needed to stand fast.

Let me give you an example from my experience.

One day, I observed a warrant officer making fun of a female soldier (he outranked the person). He initially just teased her, but in an instant with one comment, the teasing crossed the line of good taste. When he began to mention how tight her uniform was, it was obvious she was distraught. I told him to quiet down or I would report him to his supervisor for Code of Conduct violations. It was obvious that neither I nor the female soldier appreciated his sexual innuendos. He told me that this was just a little fun and not to make too much of it. He said a couple of more things and I ordered (I outranked him) him to go with me to see the supervisor. The warrant officer had two daughters and I asked him if he would appreciate someone using the same words toward his daughters. He said he would not appreciate that at all and began to understand the effects of his behavior.

You must name the truth and stand up for others. I intervened because it was the right thing to do.

The warrant officer was admonished by my supervisor and his supervisor. He apologized to everyone concerned. The bottom line is that you must hold true to your personal and organizational values. Demand that everyone be treated with respect and dignity.

---

TP: Courage demands that you make sure you are right and then forge ahead ready and willing to accept the consequences of your actions. You do this knowing you are right!

---

# CHAPTER 12
# QUESTIONS AND ANSWERS

**Question: How do I know when it is the right time to intervene in difficult situations? I don't want to lose my job.**

It is very difficult to draw a line in all situations. Let me say that you will have to decide where the line is and when you should take action. I would recommend you memorize your personal and organizational values or keep them posted near your desk for a quick review. Don't go looking for problems around those values; they will come to you quickly enough. Be sure what you will fight for and what battles you consider essential. Select your battles carefully!

**Question: Is there a way to redirect someone who is making a poor choice without being confrontational?**

Yes. First, having a good relationship with them is critical. You can tell them the truth and they will listen. Second, make sure you can connect their actions back to the organizational values when possible. Third, tie their actions back to treating all people with respect and dignity.

Another way may be to play dumb with them. Start your response to what they are doing by sharing how their actions are going against the organizational values. Assure them that you know that is not their intention, but you wanted to let them know the perceptions of their actions. This third party discussion is less confrontational but gets the point across. It gives the person time to reflect and realize they may be making a mistake.

**Question: What if my boss is constantly making fun of one employee?**

I would suggest you tell the boss about reading this book and blame your discussion on my words. This focuses the initial anger on me and the book and not on you. It does let the boss know they are not being fair in a subtle, and perhaps, less threatening manner. If this does not work, then you may have to get some organizational assistance with your human resource department or their hotline for problems.

# CHAPTER 13 – CONFIDENCE.

## SHOW CONFIDENCE IN YOUR PEOPLE.

---

"To succeed in life, you need two things: ignorance and confidence."
—*Mark Twain*

"Be courteous to all, but intimate with few, and let those few be well tried before you give them your confidence." —*George Washington*

"Leadership is solving problems. The day soldiers stop bringing you their problems is the day you have stopped leading them. They have either lost confidence that you can help or concluded you do not care. Either case is a failure of leadership." —*Colin Powell*

"I am not interested in power for power's sake, but I'm interested in power that is moral, that is right and that is good."
—*Martin Luther King, Jr.*

The very elementary step in showing confidence in your people requires you have confidence in yourself first. You must be comfortable with your job and your expertise in order to exhibit confidence in others. You must believe that you have a place in the organization. Others can tell if you have confidence in yourself and your judgment. Therefore, your self-esteem projects confidence in you. Be very careful of your ego getting in the way here.

You must avoid the appearance of arrogance and call that self-confidence. Arrogance and ego can be detriments to your self-confidence.

**TP: You must have confidence in yourself first before you can have it in others. Beware of ego and arrogance tearing down your appearance to others.**

Showing confidence, dare I say a trust (number one) in your people, requires a great deal of risk. As you work to develop people (number seven), you will have to train them, talk to them, exhibit confidence in them, and then empower them. They will know if you have confidence in them. In most cases, that confidence and trust will be returned. You must stay positive and celebrate wins of your people.

**TP: Confidence in people requires risk and trust. Publicize wins to your people and let them share in the success.**

So how do we build confidence? Please consult the chart below.

| Building Self-Confidence | Destroying Self-Confidence |
|---|---|
| A general belief in what you are doing is important | Not really understanding your role in the organization |
| Understanding the nuances of the work you have; Clear priorities | Not clearly understanding the work or priorities of work |
| Taking calculated risks to improve the organization; Following the strategic plan | Scared to make decisions and take any risks for fear of failure; Do not want attention from boss |

| | |
|---|---|
| Not afraid to share the credit when success is achieved | Deep desire to keep wins (success) and losses (failures) very secretively |
| Accepting compliments humbly but letting someone else bring it up | Looking to move forward in the organization based upon politics and not on work achievement |
| Move to rational thinking; Treating others with Respect/Dignity | Move to irrational thinking; Looking to promote self above others |

Leaders must have a general belief in what they are doing and efforts they are leading. Additionally, as we have talked about in previous chapters, there is a necessity to have some clear priorities and a way to measure success. Self-confidence comes with an appreciation of the organization, the people, and the mission. Leaders must treat all employees with respect and dignity.

I once had a friend of mine who spent enormous amounts of time ridiculing his boss and employees to make himself look better. He worked diligently on politics and kissing up (a nice way to put it) rather than just doing his job. His employees hated him and chose purposely not do what he said because he was dreadfully incompetent as a Leader. He eventually was promoted though because his boss felt sorry for him. This friend to this day does not have any self-confidence and probably never will. My friend had a great deal of ego but not self-confidence. Rather than standing by his people and his work, he would continuously criticize them. He ensured that problems were always someone else's fault. We called him the Teflon Major – nothing positive or negative would stick to him. His total lack of self-confidence worked against him in being accepted by his people. He did not make any major decisions because he lacked confidence. Don't be like that! Please!

TP: You must develop yourself and have confidence in your judgment in order to lead others.

# CHAPTER 13
# QUESTIONS AND ANSWERS

**Question: What is the difference between self-confidence and arrogance?**

| Self-Confidence | Arrogance |
|---|---|
| Good attribute | Negative attribute |
| Gained by experience, competence, and good results | Gained by believing in oneself at all costs and too much self-confidence |
| Good emotion for you and others around you | Negative emotion for people around you |
| Founded in solid relationships | Destroys relationships |
| Realistic most of the time | Unrealistic most of the time |
| Validated by results | Validated by alienation of others |
| Makes people feel good | Makes people into victims of events |
| Shows and seldom needs communication (unspoken) | Requires verbal communication |
| Does not need to boast/brag about it | Needs to boast/brag about it |
| Truthful; Based upon facts/results | False; Based upon perception |

The bottom line is that self-confidence is shown and felt by the individual and arrogance is communicated and felt by others.

**Question: How do you know if someone is arrogant or self-confident?**

The arrogant person will do the following based upon my research and experience.

1) Be very political. Arrogant people will drop names of others who are senior in the organization. They will try to make friends with higher supervisors so they can talk about something they said. They will work diligently on becoming a buddy so they can feel better than their employees.

2) Not authentic. Arrogant people really do not care about others. Decisions they make will not even consider the ramifications for lower level employees. They will not ask for ideas or suggestions from anyone except their buddies (higher level supervisors).

3) Unconcerned about rules. Rules do not apply to them especially if they have been able to align themselves with higher level supervisors. They feel as though the rules, policies, and procedures apply to others – never them. Weak buddies (higher level supervisors) will often let them take over meetings and will not hold them accountable which feeds their arrogance.

4) Condescending. Arrogant people will never accept accountability for anything. Goals and performance plans do not apply to them either. They will constantly blame outside influences for problems, most often their problems. They never make a mistake.

5) Smarter. They are always smarter than anyone else in the room. They become very frustrated when questioned or when challenged

by others. They always one-up others with more graphic stories, even if they have to make it up. They know everything about everything and will listen to no one. They are a legend in their own mind.

**Question: How can I build my own self-confidence?**

In order to build your self-confidence, you need to accomplish the following.

1) Be positive. You must develop and maintain a positive attitude by seeing all work as an opportunity to learn and become better.

2) SWOT. As we discussed earlier in the book, you will need to develop your strengths, weaknesses, opportunities, and threats to job accomplishment.

3) Mistakes. You will have to overcome your mistakes and realize we all make them. Do not linger in the past but learn and grow by the wisdom you gain.

4) Principles and Values. Make sure you evaluate your principles and values early on and remember to never sway from them. This sets the pace for all of your actions as you run problems through the filters of your principles and values.

**Question: How do I help an employee who does not realize the extent of their arrogance and alienates other members of the team?**

This is a very tough question. Arrogant people routinely do not know how to evaluate their behavior. In some organizations they have been allowed to express their arrogance without any controls. Follow the steps outlined below and hope they can self-evaluate.

1) Do your homework. Visit with your human resource professional and update yourself on current policies and procedures.

2) Monitor events. You will need to closely monitor events such as meetings, hallway discussions, employee survey results, accountability meetings, etc. to determine if arrogance is noted.

3) Document their behavior. Begin the process of documenting their arrogant behavior. Point this out to them and be firm in the discussion. This should be pointed out when it occurs or as soon as a pattern is detected.

4) Provide Counseling. Attempt to rectify their actions with counseling if possible.

5) Disciplinary Policies. You will need to carefully begin the process of disciplinary action including terminations.

# CHAPTER 14 – BE DECISIVE, PERSISTENT, AND PATIENT.

"Greatness is not a function of circumstance. Greatness, it turns out, is largely a matter of conscious choice, and discipline." —*Jim Collins*

"Most discussions of decision making assume that only senior executives make decisions or that only senior executives' decisions matter. This is a dangerous mistake." —*Peter Drucker*

"You will either step forward into growth or you will step back into safety." —*Abraham Maslow*

"Successful leaders have the courage to take action where others hesitate." —*F. A. Manske, Jr.*

"If everyone is thinking alike then somebody isn't thinking." —*Martin Luther King, Jr.*

Decision making is a basic ingredient of leadership. The ability to make decisions can have a significant impact on your personal success and the organizational success. The organizational or personal strategic plan sets the direction for every action. It is a good idea to allow subordinates to provide input into decisions, within limits, when possible and as time permits. Employee involvement equals commitment. The Leader needs to frame the conversation such as, "We are going to improve customer service, give me some input on how to do it." This frames the conversation toward improving customer service. The question is not what we are working toward but gaining their input on how best to do it.

---

TP: You must make sound decisions based upon pragmatic information. Beware of information paralysis – waiting on additional information and refusing to make a decision.

---

Let me give you a word of caution here. If everyone agrees with you as the Leader, then someone is not telling the truth. You need people to respectfully disagree with you to ensure you are looking at all opportunities for success and potential failure. If your employees begin to sound very supportive of all of your decisions (like your mother), then you have a real problem with honesty. Getting ready to hear differences of opinion it is not easy. No one is smart enough to make every decision without input and get it right every time. Do not fall into that trap and do not get angry when employees discuss other options with you. It shows a lack of confidence when you do this.

---

TP: Do not fall victim to the thought that you are always right. No one is always right!

---

I like to use a decision matrix for difficult decisions. In order to use this tool, organizations must have a strategic plan. Let's say that your boss asks you to determine the best way to get feedback from your customers. She informs you that customer service and satisfaction is critical to improve

the financial side of the business and therefore is deemed to have a higher degree of need than the other goals.

As an example, in the chart below, your part of the organization has three major goals as shown in the left column of: customer service and satisfaction, employee development, and resources management. The boss also announces that she wants this organization to do some research and determine what world class organizations do in this area. She has added the world class research into the best practice of other organizations.

Let's go on to say that the customer service and satisfaction is twice as important (x2). We will assign the numbers as follows: 5 is best for our organization to determine customer service and satisfaction, 3 is neutral, and 1 represents the worst alternative. If you had additional courses of action, always stay with odd numbers. As an example, if you had four courses of action, then 7, 5, 3, and 1 would be the numbers used and so on.

It works like this diagram below. Remember, 5 is best option, 3 is neutral, and 1 is the worst option.

| Organizational Goals – Improving Customer Service (overall goal in strategic plan) | Course of Action A- Do Nothing (determine our current action is ok now) | Course of Action B- Customer Service and Satisfaction Survey every 6 months | Course of Action C- Customer Service and Satisfaction Survey every 18 months |
|---|---|---|---|
| Customer Service and Satisfaction x2 (most important as defined by Leader) | 2 (2x1=2) (multiplied by 2) | 10 (5x2=10) (multiplied by 2) | 6 (3x2=6) (multiplied by 2) |

| Employee Development | 1 (worst option) | 5 (best option) | 3 (neutral option) |
|---|---|---|---|
| Resource Management $$$ | 5 (best option) | 1 (worst option) | 3 (neutral option) |
| World Class Organizations | 1 (worst option) | 5 (best option) | 3 (neutral option) |
| Total Points | 9 (adding all above) | 21 (adding all above) | 15 (adding all above) |

*Decision Making Chart, McGuire 2013*

Everything being equal it appears the best alternative is Course of Action B which had 21 points after points were assigned. If the organization is strapped for cash, they may select Course of Action C due to financial constraints and try that option to see if they can gain greater insight from customers. If Course of Action C does not improve customer service and satisfaction, Course of Action B may be the best alternative based upon funds available. If the organization tries the Course of Action C option, it may give the organization enough insight about Customer Service and Satisfaction. The addition of reviewing what World Class Organizations do with monitoring Customer Service and Satisfaction should encourage substantial improvements. Following world class organizations and the way they conduct business should require some research and looking outside the organization for best practice. This should help the organization get better in a meaningful way.

**TP: Organizations can make their best decisions by using the matrix with three goals from the Strategic Plan and utilizing best practices from World Class Organizations.**

The team should present the thought processes used in completing the matrix to higher level supervisors for approval. It is important that all team members be given the opportunity to participate in the explanation of the process and how the numbers were decided upon to ensure the boss understands the rationale utilized.

# CHAPTER 14
# QUESTIONS AND ANSWERS

**Question: Why is it important to follow this process for decision making?**

Organizations need to use their strategic plan to make decisions. This systematic decision making process (described above) will establish some parameters and allows everyone the same view of organizational problems. The process also highlights priorities for action.

**Question: Why can't I just make the decision on behalf of everyone?**

Smart Leaders can make minor decision quickly and on their own. When we have difficult decisions, we need to use the knowledge of everyone on the team to make sure we have the best outcome. Engaging employees in critical discussions allows for employee buy-in to improving the organization. The employees feel as though they have a say in what is important. If they are not in line with the strategic plan and organizational priorities, more education and training may be needed.

**Question: What does having patience have to do with making good decisions?**

Patience is required when the organization has a difficult decision that may have a negative consequence on the organization in relationship with customers, staff, or financial concerns to mention a few. Patience will allow some time to step back, engage your people, and truly evaluate a way forward.

# CHAPTER 15 – TAKE INTELLIGENT CALCULATED RISKS.

"Only the wisest and stupidest of men never change." —*Confucius*

"There is nothing more difficult to take in hand, more perilous to conduct, or more uncertain in its success, than to take the lead in the introduction of a new order of things. Whosoever desires constant success must change his conduct with the times." —*Machiavelli*

"People don't resist change. They resist being changed!" —*Peter Senge*

"Even though you're on the right track—you'll get run over if you just sit there." —*Will Rogers*

"Change is a necessary evil both personal and organizational. The business world is littered with people and organizations that refused to change." —*C. U. (Mac) McGuire III*

It is necessary to take some calculated risks to improve the bottom line, to improve customer service and satisfaction, and to improve employee morale. If you are in education, it takes some risk to improve student achievement, parent involvement, and teacher satisfaction. If you find yourself in health care related industries, risk can improve patient and family satisfaction and doctor and nurse satisfaction. If the employees are encouraged to makes some changes congruent with the strategic plan, then the organization can grow, the employees can develop further, and customer satisfaction can improve. Organizations and individuals in organizations must learn to fear complacency. Apathy and complacency have no place in a forward-looking, strategically driven organization.

---

TP: Calculated risks are those risks we take when the outcome may lead to organizational achievement. A review of the problem data may help us have success.

---

Sometimes to improve our chances of accelerating change and overcoming complacency, it may be necessary to change the roles of subordinates. This change in roles allows the employees to see the organization differently – through a new lens. This change in roles may include new tasks, new assignments, or new projects to address perceived deficiencies.

There are two primary reasons to change the roles of subordinates. First, the Leaders need to experience the problems of others and look at those problems with new eyes. Problems can look very simple from outside the organization but daunting from the inside if there are resource limitations, cultural boundaries, and organizational chart limitations. This changing of roles allows new ideas to be generated and a new perspective. It is much harder to criticize others when you have to walk in their shoes. When subordinates have the opportunity to look at the job and the organization differently, they grow.

Secondly, changing roles/tasks can reenergize employees and give them something new to experience. This engages grey matter and helps them feel fresher about work. It may even cause them to be attracted to their work again anew. This period of refreshment can lead to new ideas and enhancements at work and at home. We all need something new in our lives periodically to reboot us.

---

**TP: Sometimes it may be necessary to change roles of individuals and Leaders for a new look at problems. This can generate new ideas and reduce complacency.**

---

Beer's (2007) change formula inspired me to think differently about change and how to address it in a positive way. His formula was as follows: Amount of Change = (Dissatisfaction X Model X Success) > Cost of Change http://www.ibscdc.org/executive-interviews/Q&A_with_Michael_Beer_6.htm.

From his formula and my experience, I thought of change a little differently. There are a number of change formulas out there but I like Change = DOPE>C. I describe it this way.

Change is equal to being:

D stands for being Dissatisfied with the way things are. This could be in your professional life or your personal life. In either case, YOU must be dissatisfied with where you have been, where you are, and where you see yourself going in the future. No one can make you dissatisfied – that is your responsibility.

O relates to the Options you have. List the options you have which may correspond to the opportunities portion of your SWOT we mentioned earlier. As we get older, we may have fewer opportunities to make drastic changes in our professions/careers and, in some cases, in our personal lives. The professional limitations are sometimes real and sometimes perceived, but we can make real changes in our personal lives at any time.

P stands for a Plan. We need a plan of action to make the changes a reality. We need mentors in our life to help us decide about how we should plan as well as assist with milestones for achievement. This plan should be in writing. You heard that right – in writing so you can clearly see every day if you are moving toward your goals or not.

E stands for Execution. If we have a plan but you never execute the plan – it is worthless. Therefore, execution is critical to using the plan effectively.

The D, O, P, E must be more powerful than C which is the cost to you. This cost is financial, time management (stay whelmed), family trials, work obligations, and the difficulty of the plan. Psychological, mental, and physical costs are also included. The costs and sacrifices you have to make to accomplish the change must be worth it in your mind.

---

**TP: There are sacrifices you will have to make to accomplish changes. No career or personal change occurs without some associated pain. Consider having an accountability partner (someone who can keep you in pursuit of your change) to help you with your effort.**

---

Here are two questions to consider about taking risks and making changes in your professional as well as your personal life.

✓ What is the one thing you need to change at work to make your organization more effective (look at the strategic plan for guidance)?

✓ What is the one thing you need to change in your personal life to make you happier and fulfill your dreams?

The answer to these two questions will put you on the right path.

TP: Address these two questions and perhaps you are about to make some positive changes for you and your life. Cautionary note: Don't wait too long and get started today!

# CHAPTER 15
# QUESTIONS AND ANSWERS

Question: How do I really know when the time is right to make a change or take an intelligent risk so I don't have regrets later in life?

I wish I could answer this question easily, but the answer is elusive. First and foremost, you have to be dissatisfied at work or at home or on a particular routine task to want to change it. You must see the benefits of looking at the problem another way. If the dissatisfaction is significant enough on your life/work, you begin to explore options and consider the requirements of doing something about the dissatisfaction.

Mentors can play a huge role here in assisting with your dissatisfaction. Mentors can give you glimpses of alternatives you may want to explore. Remember to utilize your SWOT (mentioned earlier) in deciding what you want to change/risk and how quickly you want to do that.

Finally, the exploration of a change or intelligent risk should make you feel uncomfortable and somewhat fearful. Doing something differently from your normal is a scary endeavor but can be a glorious opportunity. This new opportunity can lead to a new life, one with great enjoyment and very fulfilling. You will never know unless you explore your opportunities.

Question: What if it is evident that my organization needs to make changes but my supervisors think change is too much trouble?

The previous discussed dissatisfaction holds true for your supervisors as well as with you personally. If the changes are not presented as the best option, the supervisors may not make the change. Your job is to convince with research, data, and passion that the change is necessary and can lead to substantial success. Unless you can convince your supervisors of this success, the change will probably never occur.

Sometimes it is a good idea to bring in an outside person to help describe the change. As an example, my consulting career is built around helping organizations and individuals grow and become better based upon the organizational and individual definitions of success. I work with a number of improvement models but enjoy the Baldrige Criteria for Performance Improvement because of its holistic nature. So if you wanted to change direction of the organization, you might contact me or another consultant to present what organizations are doing that follow this model. My first book was about those improvements in the Executive Guide to the Baldrige Criteria (McGuire, 2007).

Question: How do I gain support from others (family, co-workers, etc.) to help me with my changes?

Family. This is a tough question if the family does not talk often about dreams and needs. Your spouse can be a major contributor to the change and can be a huge stumbling block. You need to voice what you want to accomplish in life and have the spouse affirm your desire. Now they need to be honest with you about your dreams and whether they are realistic. Assuming the change is realistic;

your family should support you after you have done your homework about the requirements in time, money, and effort.

Co-workers. You will have to convince your co-workers that a change is needed. Much like the conversation in question 1, bringing in an outside consultant can be a big help IF it is the right one. Attending classes with co-workers away from the workplace can spur changes or identify needs for making some changes at work.

Whoever is in your sphere of influence and those who influence you must come alongside of you. You have to convince them of the necessity of the change and how it will make things better. In all instances, you have to paint a picture of the change and put your loved ones, co-workers, or friends in the picture in order to obtain buy-in from them.

# CHAPTER 16 – SENSE OF URGENCY/PRIORITIES

"I have been impressed with the urgency of doing. Knowing is not enough; we must apply. Being willing is not enough; we must do."
—*Leonardo da Vinci*

"You must take action now that will move you towards your goals. Develop a sense of urgency in your life." —*H. Jackson Brown, Jr.*

"Committing your goals to paper increases the likelihood of achieving them by one-thousand percent. I found every single successful person I've ever spoken to had a turning point. The turning point was when they made a clear, specific unequivocal decision that they were not going to live like this anymore; they were going to achieve success. Some people make that decision at 15 and some people make it at 50, and most people never make it at all." —*Brian Tracy*

Urgency and priorities are intricately linked. We will never create a sense of urgency (what to work on first) unless we have data indicating current status. Urgency is the need to accomplish high-priority work. As the Leader, you will have to provide a sense of urgency in order to get your people to focus on the right priorities. The urgency may center on the bottom line for businesses in their profit, student performance and teacher satisfaction for educators, or patient, family, and employee satisfaction results for health care professionals. A sense of urgency normally follows low performance on key priorities at work or negative results validated by accurate data collection.

Low performance requires a sense of urgency driven by Leader expectations to fix it. Whatever it is your organization has low performance in, measure it, track it over time, and never accept less than excellence. Carefully consider what tasks to push with the sense of urgency (can't wait mentality). There must be deadlines with delegation.

It is critical to drive measured performance: measure goals individually, by group, and organizationally (top to bottom). Measure it! Segmentation is critical so you can determine where weaknesses in performance may exist. To give the reader an idea about segmentation, some examples are as follows below.

| For-Profit Business and Manufacturing Considerations | Type of products<br>Geographical areas for marketing/selling<br>Employee satisfaction/engagement<br>Salesperson statistics on sales by region/area |
| --- | --- |
| Educational Institutions (K-12) and higher education | Student performance by campus and by teacher<br>Campus performance by principal and by teacher<br>Teacher satisfaction by campus<br>Family satisfaction by campus<br>Community satisfaction by areas |
| Health Care | Patient satisfaction by floor (hospital) by staff area<br>Family satisfaction<br>Community satisfaction<br>Doctor satisfaction<br>Employee satisfaction<br>Nurse satisfaction by tenure |

| Not-for-Profit | Donor satisfaction this year vs. last year<br>Donor giving by year by group<br>Types of products offered<br>Products supported |
|---|---|

TP: A sense of urgency is critical to focus work on the right priorities. As the Leader, you set the pace or you accept excuses and give up! You (Leader) are the catalyst for success or failure.

Urgency is critical to mission accomplishment. In one of my organizations the Commander (my boss) tasked all his subordinate Generals with the requirement to improve recruiting and retention. He told them this effort was urgent and failure would not be accepted. Numbers would improve in recruiting and retention or people would be terminated.

To check the data, the Commander (my boss) asked me to retrieve some data regarding the performance of a subordinate General concerning the number one goal of recruiting and retention. I was asked to collect and synthesize the data for the prior three years on our key performance measures (urgency and priority) before the subordinate was allowed to continue in the Army. It was evident by looking at the data that the subordinate General was not doing a good job of Leading (Big L) on recruitment or retention. His numbers were dreadful. It was apparent by the numbers that he did not have the sense of urgency, could not do the job, or did not care. Bottom line, he was not effective. The data spoke volumes about how bad the subordinate General was and how his lack of Leadership was obviously limiting success.

TP: The data will inform you of your sense of urgency being addressed, success in accomplishing priority work, and the success of your subordinates. While you may feel as though you are doing a credible job, the data may suggest otherwise. Keep data close to you and monitor success and failure carefully.

Again, the sense of urgency (what needs to be done) and your priorities work in consonance with each other. You (Leader) must set the urgency and the right priorities for the office.

The most urgent tasks should be very clear to all subordinates. In addressing urgency and priorities, I like the A, B, C's for simplicity. All tasks should be written down and worked from the list. Urgent tasks/priorities are identified in work as A's must be accomplished today before leaving work. This number of A's should not exceed five in most cases. If there are more than five A's, additional stress may felt by your subordinates. B's are those tasks needing completion within 48-72 hours. The C's must be finished this week or this month.

The Leader should establish those priorities and reinforce the sense of urgency and priorities each and every day by walking around and talking to their people. If geography is an issue (you have some remote employees that are not in the same building), a phone call and email should do the trick to ensure the priorities are being addressed even at remote locations. Leaders need to measure success continually on all tasks but especially the urgent ones.

TP: Leaders set the sense of urgency and the priorities of work or not. If you (Leader) are not setting clear priorities – you are wrong. Everyone who works for you should be able to recite the top three most urgent priorities. If not, the Leader has not done a good job in listing the priorities.

Leaders must ensure each employee has an Individual Development Plan (IDP) or Personal Development Plan (PDP) supporting their urgent tasks/ priorities of work, their personal goals at work, and what education and training is needed to develop them further toward organizational success.

---

TP: Leaders must ensure the most important work is done first, period. If you fail to establish priorities, firefighting (running from one priority to the next) will rule the day!

---

# CHAPTER 16
# QUESTIONS AND ANSWERS

**Question: Are all priorities considered urgent? How do I know?**

The most critical factor in selecting what priorities are the most urgent is to base them on the strategic planning document. Review your vision, mission, and goals. What should be the most important and essential priorities IF we are going to aggressively accomplish the strategic plan?

**Question: What if my supervisor does not give me priorities? How many priorities are reasonable?**

In the absence of a strategic plan, you will have to approach your boss and discuss their priorities. If they tell you everything is a priority, you are in a difficult position. If you are not clear after a discussion with your boss about the right priorities, consider deliberation and then return to the boss by taking the boss your perceived list of top three priorities. This list should be thoughtfully considered. Hopefully, you can get some agreement on your list or perhaps approval. This list is your list of top priorities.

If that does not work, the Leader needs to carefully select the top three priorities based upon the organization and make sure to publicize the priorities to all employees. Additionally, all priorities should be included in the employee and organizational evaluation instruments.

The key here is to do something about letting all employees know what is important and checking on those top three priorities.

**Question: How do I help my staff understand the urgency in their work?**

In one word, the answer is – repetition. The Leader must continually place the priorities up front in all discussions around organizational and individual performance. In Roundings for Outcomes, the Leader needs to emphasize the criticality of working the right priorities. Do not allow individuals to go aimlessly and work on what they perceive to be the priorities.

It will also help to have a chart in the office to track success and failure of some predetermined priorities. Be careful here about the information being proprietary and the need to keep this from competitors.

# CHAPTER 17 – BE LOYAL.

"The scholar does not consider gold and jade to be precious treasures, but loyalty and good faith.   —*Confucius*

"If you live to be 100, I hope I live to be 100 minus 1 day, so I never have to live without you."   —*Winnie the Pooh*

"Lack of loyalty is one of the major causes of failure in every walk of life."
—*Napoleon Hill*

"You've got to give loyalty down, if you want loyalty up."
—*D. T. Regan*

"When we are debating an issue, loyalty means giving me your honest opinion, whether you think I'll like it or not. Disagreement, at this state, stimulates me. But once a decision is made, the debate ends. From that point on, loyalty means executing the decision as if it were your own."
—*General Colin Powell*

Loyalty is defined as "the state or quality of being loyal; faithfulness to commitments or obligations; faithful adherence to a sovereign, government, leader, cause, etc." (Office Ethics Columns, n.d.). Does this mean blind loyalty which is so most often associated with those born in the 1950s or 1960s? Or has the definition of loyalty changed? I think it may have changed.

Some say there is a new type of loyalty for today's workplace (http://www.office-ethics.com/columns/loyalty.html). The new loyalty is not as unconditional as loyalty has been in the past. The unconditional loyalty or blind loyalty meant underlings supported their bosses at all costs and would rise or fall based on the actions of the boss. The new loyalty requires a degree of professionalism within a set of standards that are different for each organization. These standards of loyalty may be different for subcultures in various parts of the organization also. We must attempt each day to take care of your boss, your organization, and yourself.

TP: Understand what loyalty means to your boss and what the expectations are in your organization. Do they really want you to tell them the truth or just support them blindly. Are there any standards of loyalty?

In my past, I worked for a number of bosses who really thought loyalty meant telling them what they wanted to hear. Agreeing with them regardless of what they said or suggested was their definition of true loyalty. That could not be further from the truth.

General Powell's quote at the beginning of the chapter was brought home to me by Lieutenant General (Ret.) Danny James, a previous good boss, who thought the best definition of loyalty was for staff to be completely honest in their conversations to allow him to make the best decisions at the time.

TP: I hope that you can tell your boss the truth without having to agree with them all the time. I hope your boss encourages disagreements (time to communicate different opinions) as a way to look at other options for difficult decisions.

All organizations need some "Talking Time and Walking Time." I used this during my tenure as a Battalion Commander in the Army and it works extremely well. The "Talking Time" is where I need and in fact solicit your opinion about the decision to be made. Major Williams, my executive officer, was the very best at this. We would and could talk about issues and he would tell me why my ideas might not be the best way to address the problem based upon our strategic plan or Army values. There were many occasions where Major Williams convinced me to change my mind to make the best decision for the organization. The "talking time" was then over and it was time to execute the decision or "Walking Time." "Walking Time" is the execution of the plans based upon the final decision. Major Williams was one of the best at giving me good, honest advice about the best decision, and we worked well together. "Walking Time" meant there was no more "Talking Time." Talking time was over and execution was beginning. Regardless of the decision, Major Williams supported my decision. He understood loyalty, and I sincerely appreciated his loyalty to me.

---

TP: I highly recommend you use "Talking Time" to gather data/information regarding a difficult upcoming decision. After a time to discuss the options, "Walking Time" begins. This "Walking Time" should not lead to further discussion and everyone must execute the decision made by the boss. Listen and solicit information for a decision, if time permits, with your people and then make a decision for the organization.

---

You must be careful not to be seen as competitive to your boss. This is self-defeating. If you have a boss that is very insecure, be careful how you approach them. This competition is often spurred by being an extravert with an introverted boss. The introverted person will most often be in awe of the extraverted directness.

---

**TP: Do not get into a competitive showdown with your boss.**

---

Be loyal to your people. Be aggressive in serving them, watching out for them, and working with them as necessary. They need to know you honestly care about them and will step up to protect them from all comers if necessary. If you lose a debate about employee protection with your boss, that is ok, but it should be after a discussion of what it will do to your people. You owe your people support if they are following your decisions.

---

**TP: Aggressively serve your people.**

---

You also need to treat every employee with respect and dignity. You must do this. All of your employees as well as others in the organization need to see you in a positive light. You can never tell who may be your boss in the future.

---

**TP: Everyone who works in your organization deserves respect and dignity. EVERYONE!**

---

Many years ago as a private (enlisted man), I brought a load of supplies to a military warehouse, and I had not completed the paper work properly. A Sergeant Major with over twenty years of service was furious with me, called me names, and told me to drive over 250 miles back to my home location since I did not complete the paper work properly. I told him I was new and did not know how to complete it. I requested some assistance so I could do what was necessary to complete the paperwork properly. He not only refused my request but ordered me back into the truck and did not care that I had just driven over 250 miles that day (long day at 55 miles per hour in a military 2 ½ ton truck. Six years later, I became his supervisor as a Captain (he was still a sergeant major). He remembered me and profusely apologized to me for what he had done to me several years earlier. I told him that I would not allow him to treat anyone like that again and we eventually became friends. I told him IF I caught him treating someone as he had treated me, there would be a price to pay.

---

**TP: Treat everyone with respect and dignity. Be careful how you treat people, those people could become your boss one day.**

---

Be loyal to your boss. You may have a good boss or you may have a bad boss; either way . . . be Loyal. Enjoy the good bosses because the bad ones are out there. Make sure that you are not conspiring against your boss whether you like them or not. You cannot win by trying to destroy or hurt your boss.

---

**TP: Rise above all controversies and always be loyal to your boss.**

---

Be sure not to become too close to one of your employees. You are a boss and not a buddy to your employees. Let me say that again for some of you. YOU are a Boss and not a Buddy! The organization pays you to be a boss and not a buddy. Do not become close friends with your employees as it will lead to later problems. You need to be very careful if you go to lunch or other organizational functions with them. If you do go with them after work or at lunch during the work day, you may be saying to other employees that this person is more important to me than you. You could be destroying your team rather than building it. Do not play favorites at work! Having a buddy at work rather than an employee could be detrimental to team and individual development. It may cloud your ability to discipline or terminate an employee. I know this paragraph is repetitive and that was intentional!

TP: Beware of becoming too close to one of your employees and destroying team chemistry. You are to build a team, not destroy one. Remember you can mentor subordinates, but keep your professional distance from becoming a buddy relationship.

# CHAPTER 17
# QUESTIONS AND ANSWERS

**Question: How can you be loyal to a boss that is not loyal to you?**

I face this question often in my travels. Be very careful in this type of situation. First, do some self-reflection and decide if you think your boss is disloyal. On what are you basing your suspicion of disloyalty? Is it based on one event or a long-standing view of disloyalty?

If you are convinced with data that your boss is disloyal to you, is it just to you? Is the boss disloyal to others in the office? Once you have honestly determined that your boss is disloyal just to you or to everyone, begin the process of trying to show your boss loyalty.

If your boss is disloyal, you need to work hard for them but be careful in what you do. Back up your work. Be careful how far you will go in taking risks. Evaluate work knowing that you may not get any support for your actions.

Keep your head down!

**Question: Isn't loyalty a two-way street?**

Yes it is. Loyalty is one of those character traits you must give in order to receive. Are you doing your part? Loyal to boss, subordinates, customers, and peers? It starts with you.

**Question: Can you actually be loyal to your actual work?**

Yes. You must keep your commitments at work. Be very careful if you say you will do a task in a certain timeframe and then don't do it. You must be faithful to your work.

# Chapter 18 – Listen.

"Courage is what it takes to stand up and speak; courage is also what it takes to sit down and listen." *—Winston Churchill*

"It is the province of knowledge to speak and it is the privilege of wisdom to listen." *—Oliver Wendell Holmes*

"The greatest compliment that was ever paid me was when one asked me what I thought, and attended to my answer." *—Henry David Thoreau*

"Seek first to understand, then to be understood." *—Stephen R. Covey*

"To say that a person feels listened to means a lot more than just their ideas get heard. It's a sign of respect. It makes people feel valued." *—Deborah Tannen*

"Without credible communication, and a lot of it, the hearts and minds of others are never captured." *—John P. Kotter*

Some research indicates we listen at best about 25% of the time (Haney, 1979). This research was a study of over 8,000 people in businesses, hospitals, universities, and military and government entities. The emphasis for the Leader is to take the time to listen and understand the framing of the problem. Look for the root cause and attack the problem there.

---

TP: We don't listen as well as we think we do.

---

I really like Covey's (1989) habit number five "Seek first to understand, then to be understood." I have added that you do not have to agree with the conversation. In my military and consulting career, it is amazing to listen to someone make a proposal to you and then automatically expect you to agree with them. You don't have to do that! I would like to add another part to Covey's habit number five . . . "you do not have to agree." If you are the Leader, you must take all things into consideration and determine if, in some cases, you have the resources and capacity to have the proposed idea work. So you do need to listen but you do not have to agree.

---

**TP: Leaders need to continually develop and improve their listening skills. Leaders should listen to the entire conversation, ask questions, restate, provide feedback, and then decide if the proposal/idea is capable of working in the organization with the resources available.**

---

Believe it or not, Leaders need problems as we have discussed earlier and should deal with problems as soon as possible. Leaders need problems and people with problems to validate our higher level of income and our organization position. The organization counts on us to solve problems at our level and to make the best use of resources while increasing individual capability and capacity (although we normally work more hours).

---

TP: We need people with problems to validate us and our position in the organizational structure. Base decisions on three factors: mission requirement, resources, and employee capacity and capability. Mission always, always, comes first.

---

Leaders should listen to problem descriptions and ask questions. At the conclusion (when you think you know the root cause of the problem), ask the employee to suggest two solutions. If the two solutions are not reasonable or even close to being acceptable, you may not be doing a good job developing that person to fully understand the requirements of the organization (back to Chapter 7). If the two solutions suggested will work and are in line with the organizational strategic plan and goals, then you have done a good job in developing your people. Hopefully, you can select one of their solutions or accept one, with some modification, which will lead to employee buy-in.

---

TP: If you get good solutions, great job. Your people probably understand organization requirements and your emphasis is paying dividends. If you get dumb solutions to problems, then you are not doing your key job of developing your workforce. Very few, and I do mean very few, problems have only one solution: your job is to choose the best solution at that specific time.

---

Here are some of my listening techniques developed over time and based upon a myriad of research articles.

1. Stay focused on the person making the comments. Treat each listening event as if there will be a test over what they are saying. Do not attempt to do anything else except focus on each word, the word definition, and the idea expressed.

2. Ask plenty of questions. The number one way in which to learn and understand a conversation is to ask questions. Do not be confrontational and be careful of your negative body language.

3. <u>Give feedback</u>. Tell them what you thought you heard them say. Ask if what you heard, in your words, is really what they meant to say.

4. <u>Body language</u>. Be careful of negative and positive body language until you think you truly understand what they are saying.

5. <u>Let them complete their thoughts</u>. Let them completely describe their thoughts (this is not my strong suit; hope you are better than me). Do not interrupt and think you have heard the thought prematurely.

6. <u>You don't have to agree</u>. Leaders need to cognitively understand that they do not have to agree with the person even if the idea presented is the best one you have ever heard. Again, resources and capacities are necessary for execution. The devil is truly in the details.

---

**TP: Listening truly is an art. Work at improving this critical skill set which will enable the leader to fully address key problems.**

---

# CHAPTER 18
# QUESTIONS AND ANSWERS

Comment/Question: My boss never listens to me, even when my idea may be the best for the organization. How can I do a better job of communicating my ideas?

Sometimes people are introverted, reticent to speak out loud, or mild-mannered. You may also have a lack of confidence with some bosses or other people who may be in the meeting about decisions. You may be a deep-thinker and it takes some processing time before you are ready to comment. All of the aforementioned can have a significant impact on your ability to be heard. Loud people, right or wrong, get heard and are appreciated or not.

If you are introverted, reticent or mild-mannered, you may have to step out and be more open about your thoughts. This holds true if you have a lack of confidence too. Bosses should be able to draw you into the conversation if you have something to say but are reluctant to do so when they notice you are not contributing. Sad to say some bosses are not that observant.

If you are a deep-thinker, one tactic you may want to use is to suggest you be able to collect some data and do some research before addressing the issue at hand. This will allow you some time to compose your thoughts.

**Question: How do I respond to an employee who gets their feelings hurt if I don't use their idea?**

This is always a concern. We need to treat every employee with respect and dignity as we have discussed previously. You must be able to take a part of their idea and thank them for their contribution. Another way is to praise them for their idea and tell them that idea was used to come up with the best solution. Brainstorming is a way to address problems in a non-threatening way and allow a free-flow of information and ideas.

**Question: What does positive and negative body language look like?**

This is a very difficult question to address in that what I may perceive as negative may in fact be positive body language and vice versa. Let's deal with some of the issues. As you review the list below, where do you agree and disagree. Body language and how to read someone is highly debatable as to which is which. Evaluate yourself!

| Body Part | Positive | Negative |
|---|---|---|
| Face | Relaxed, open | Anxious, tight lipped |
| Eye Contact | Make eye contact with the speaker, focused on speaker | Eyes on surroundings, focused around room, distracted |
| Movement | Arms open, warm, non-threatening | Arms closed, threatening posture |
| Mouth | Smiling | Frowning |

| Head | Directed to person | Shifting around the room as with the eye contact above |
|---|---|---|
| Legs/Feet | Open and relaxed, hands in pockets indicated relaxed | Legs close together, hands on hips, close to sides |

# CHAPTER 19 – DEDICATED, AVAILABLE, AND OPTIMISTIC.

"You need to get happy in the same pants you got mad in."
—*Grandma McGuire*

"There is only one boss, the customer. And he can fire everybody in the company from the chairman on down, simply by spending his money somewhere else." —*Sam Walton*

"I've always found that the speed of the boss is the speed of the team."
—*Lee Iacocca*

"Leaders need to be optimists. Their vision is beyond the present."
—*Rudy Giuliani*

"The best leader is the one who has sense enough to pick good men to do what he wants done, and self-restraint enough to keep from meddling with them while they do it." —*Theodore Roosevelt*

"A good leader is a person who takes a little more than his share of the blame and a little less than his share of the credit." —*John C. Maxwell*

*Let me ask an essential question to determine* your commitment to the organization where you work. Are you a prisoner or a volunteer at work? When I ask this question during my seminars, I am often told of the impact it has on participants. The participants usually do not think of their professional life in these terms. If you are a prisoner, you are frustrated, angry some of the time, and feel unappreciated most of the time. You are in the wrong job and perhaps the wrong profession. If you are a volunteer, you are in the right place vocationally. You are energized in your work and relish the next day. This question is also valid in your personal life. Are you dedicated to your work? Are you living a life of misery or a life of happiness?

---

TP: Are you a prisoner or volunteer at work? Why? Is it you or the job? Is it your family situation? What do you need to do to improve your situation?

---

Let me also suggest the grass is not always greener on the other side of the fence and the water bill may be higher. Don't always assume that life will be better elsewhere. As an example, I had one young lady ask me to help her find other employment. She informed me she hated working for the government in a 40 hour per week job with low income and wanted to go into corporate America. We found her a position with a large corporation. This job paid her substantially more but required her to work 65 hours a week rather than 40-45 hours. She soon discovered the additional salary was not worth the time she had to spend away from family.

---

TP: You may need to count your blessings from time to time and realize that your situation may not be as bad as you think it is. However, if you discover the situation is as bad as you say it is; it may be time for a new adventure.

---

Leaders need to be available. I love going to the coast – especially the Texas Coast. I know some of you would say that is not a real coast but it is for me. I love everything about it except for those seagulls who continually fly around and mess up my car. On one of my trips it hit me – that is just like a "seagull" boss I had. He would fly into the office and mess up everyone's day and then fly back out. He was never there for the actual work or to support others during a time of extremely hard work. He was a politician and did not work much. He even took naps during the day and his boss allowed the naps. Now, back to the seagulls. When a storm rolls onto the coast, the seagulls fly up or down the coast or inland away from the storm. After the storm, they are back messing on my car. Like the seagulls, my seagull boss http://www.urbandictionary.com/define.php?term=seagull%20boss would fly in and mess up everything (new priorities) and then fly out. If problems (storms) developed, he could not be found. After the problem (storm) was resolved, he was back messing up everything again. Leaders should never have the "Seagull Mentality Boss." Stay with your people during hard times and work with them on the serious times on difficult problems (storms).

There is an old military maxim stating Leaders should never leave the troops in the field. Leaders provide protection so the employees (soldiers) can do their work.

---

TP: Stay away from the "Seagull Mentality Boss." Work with your people not against them. They are on your side and vice versa. Never leave your people at the office when they need your help! Leaders should be very careful not to mess up or add unnecessary work at any time. There is enough work at your location to keep everyone busy. Stay focused and with your people when times are tough.

---

Leaders should be optimistic and believe in you, your boss, your organization, and the fact that you personally are making a difference. If you cannot feel that, you are in the wrong place or perhaps you need to view work differently. Being optimistic and having a positive attitude can take you through work storms better than anything.

---

**TP: Leaders must remain optimistic and maintain a positive attitude.**

---

This wraps up this book. As a summation of the 19 Tips and Techniques, I believe this is a time to introduce the eleven U. S. Army Leadership Principles (U. S. Army, 1983) and a short narrative describing them. I really believe in these principles and they continue to help me today in my teaching and in my consulting work. These principles are essential whether you are in an educational environment, health care, or business endeavors and can be easily adapted to your situation and industry.

| Principles of Leadership | My Narrative About the Army Principles of Leadership |
|---|---|
| #1 Know Yourself; Seek Self Improvement | Develop a plan to keep your strengths and improve on your weaknesses. Continually work on strengthening your brand. Remember in the airplane emergency oxygen mask drop, we have to take care of ourselves first in order to help others. Take care of YOU! |
| #2 Be Technically Proficient | Not only do we know our duties and responsibilities, we know all those of our team members, and we look to our leaders and concern ourselves with learning their duties and responsibilities. |
| #3 Seek Responsibility; Take Responsibility for Your Actions | We are not satisfied with performing just our duties to the best of our abilities, we look to grow and seek further challenges, and always, when in charge, accept the consequences of our decisions, absorb the negative, and pass on the praises. All of the people who work for you are yours – good and bad. Take care of them and treat them with respect and dignity! |

| #4 – Make Sound, Timely Decisions | Leaders must be able to reason under the most critical conditions and decide quickly what action to take. Listen to your people and solicit ideas for improvements when and where possible. You do not have to make all the decisions by yourself. |
| --- | --- |
| #5 – Set the Example | No aspect of leadership is more powerful. Our personal example affects people more than any amount of instruction or form of discipline. We are the role model. We must walk our talk. |
| #6 – Know Your Personnel; Look Out for Their Well Being | Leaders must know and understand those being led. When individuals trust you, they will willingly work to help accomplish any mission. You have to truly understand their capabilities and their capacities. Be sure to ask the right people to do the right job and train them well. Take care of them and their well-being. |
| #7 – Keep Your Followers Informed | Our team members expect us to keep them informed, and where and when possible, to explain the reasons behind requirements and decisions. Information encourages initiative, improves teamwork and enhances morale. |
| #8 – Develop A Sense of Responsibility In Your Followers | The members of a team will feel a sense of pride and responsibility when they successfully accomplish a new task given them. When we delegate responsibility to our followers, we are indicating that we trust them. Make sure you take the time to develop your people. |
| #9 – Ensure Each Task is Understood, Supervised, and Accomplished | Team members must know the standard. Supervising lets us know the task is understood and lets our team members know we care about mission accomplishment and about them. Your people will do well in those areas you explain well, train well, and monitor well. Make sure the employees understand the priorities of work. |

| #10 – Build a Team | Leaders develop a team spirit that motivates team members to work with confidence and competence. Because mission accomplishment is based on teamwork, it is evident the better the team, the better the team will perform the task. |
| --- | --- |
| #11 – Employ Your Team In Accordance With Its Capabilities | A leader must use sound judgment when employing the team (deciding on the priorities of work and who will accomplish the tasks better). Failure is not an option. By employing the team properly, in accordance with their individual capacity and capabilities, we insure mission accomplishment to the highest effectiveness. |

# CHAPTER 19
# QUESTIONS AND ANSWERS

Question: How do I stay dedicated if the organization has lost its focus on the priorities?

Do not lose your focus. If the organization is leaving the priorities, you need to stay the course. This may be done quietly or more vocal if you perceive yourself to be the conscience of the organization.

If you have a strategic plan and believe the organization has left it, post the plan in a conspicuous place and refer to it often in daily work. This action may redirect your boss if they have unintentionally left the priorities.

If the boss does not want to follow the priorities, there is not much you can do other than hold to the priorities at your desk. Perhaps, you may want to check your networks for other employment opportunities.

Question: How do I know if I am a prisoner in my job or personal life? What should I do if I find that I am a prisoner?

You will need to do some self-reflection. I highly recommend you find a trusted ally, perhaps a mentor, to lay out your current situation honesty and without whining. After that, ask if they have any questions or advice on your next steps.

More specifically, if you are a prisoner in your personal life, the self-reflection can be done with a minister/pastor/priest, mentor, counselor, or best friend. Be careful here that the minister may not truly understand your condition such as consideration of a divorce. A counselor may be needed for contemplation of this action. Divorce will forever change your life – forever. Children will be changed. I do not support divorce but sometimes that is the only alternative, especially in the case of physical or mental abuse.

In your work life, perhaps you could solicit a transfer to another area of the organization that fits your skill sets better. You may need to acquire more education in order to make this shift, but do not let hard work frighten you. Remember that opportunity is something more people would recognize if it did not come disguised as hard work.

**Question: How do I address someone in my organization that is a "seagull boss"?**

Not a lot you can do here unless your relationship with your boss will allow honest conversations and you can present this book in the discussion. If you can bring it up and impress your boss about the actions they take and the way it looks to the employees/team, they may be able to make a change.

**Question: How can the military leadership principles help me in my organization? We are not the military.**

I can only tell you that the military has been studying leadership hundreds of years. What works best and what does not work. This study has revealed those principles. Application of those principles can help any organization and any person. As I teach leadership development programs, the military principles can be applied to any organization anywhere.

# CONCLUSION

In conclusion, I hope and pray that this book will help each of you become a better Leader. May you be stronger for reading it!

# References

Academy of Achievement. (n.d.). Rosa Parks. Retrieved from http://www.achievement.org/autodoc/page/par0int-1 dated Jun 19, 2012.

Armstrong, M. (2006). Kogan Page. Retrieved from http://books.google.com/books?id=GTSmxN66g4cC&pgis=1 dated Jun 5, 2012.

Army.Mil Features. (2012). The Army values. Retrieved from http://www.army.mil/values/index.html dated Jun 15, 2012.

Arvin, D. (2008). The management map: Navigation tools for the new manager. Plano, TX, ManageSmart Publications.

Beer, M. (2007). Interview with Michael Beer on Change Management. Retrieved from http://www.ibscdc.org/executive-interviews/Q&A_with_Michael_Beer_6.htm not dated.

Bell, C. R. (2002). Managers as mentors. San Francisco, CA: Berrett-Koehler Publishers, Inc.

Bennis, W. & Nanus, B. (1985; 1997; 2003). Leaders: Strategies for taking charge. NY: HarperCollins.

Bennis, W. (1989). On becoming a leader. NY: Persus Books.

Biblios.com. (2012). Proverbs 29:18 KJV. Retrieved from http://kingjbible.com/proverbs/29.htm.

Bloom, B. S. (1956). Taxonomy of educational objectives handbook 1: The cognitive domain. N Y: David McKay Co Inc.

Covey, S. R. (1989; 2004). The 7 habits of highly effective people. NY: Simon & Schuster, Inc.

Dictionary.com. (n.d.). Ethics definition. Retrieved from http://dictionary.reference.com/browse/ethics June 5, 2012.

Dictionary.com. (n.d.). Honesty definition. Retrieved from http://dictionary.reference.com/browse/honesty?s=t May 22, 2012.

Dictionary.com. (n.d.). Integrity definition. Retrieved from http://dictionary.reference.com/browse/integrity?s=t May 22, 2012.

DeVos, R. M. (2008). Ten powerful phrases for positive people. NY: Hachette Book Group.

Encyclopedia of Business. (n.d.). Goals and goal setting. Retrieved from http://www.referenceforbusiness.com/management/Ex-Gov/Goals-and-Goal-Setting.html#b dated Jun 7, 2012.

Frankl, V. E. (1959). Man's search for meaning. NY: Pocket Books.

Galford, R. M. & Drapeau, A. S. (2002). The trusted leader: Bringing out the best in your people and your company. NY: Simon & Schuster, Inc., pp. 8-16.

Glasser, I. (n.d.). Branch Rickey and Jackie Robinson: Precursors of the Civil Rights Movement. Retrieved from http://www.worldandi.com/newhome/public/2003/march/mtpub.asp dated Jun 19, 2012.

Goleman, D. (2006). Emotional intelligence. NY: Bantam Books.

Greenleaf, F. (1977; 1991, 2002). Servant leadership: A journey into the nature of legitimate power & greatness. Mahwah, NJ: Paulist Press.

Haden, J. (2012, Mar 28). The 9 elements of highly effective employee praise. Inc. Retrieved from http://www.inc.com/jeff-haden/the-9-elements-of-highly-effective-employee-praise.html May 21, 2012.

Haney, W. V. (1979). Communication and interpersonal relations Homewood, IL: Irwin.

Johnson, R. (1995, Sept/Oct). Rearranging deck chairs on the Titanic. Bulletin of the Atomic Scientists. Retrieved from http://books.google.com/books?id=gsAAAAMBAJ&pg=PA11&dq=chairs+on+the+Titanic&hl=en&sa=X&ei=L_K_T6KHLury2QWSoaGPDQ&ved=0CGMQ6AEwBA#v=onepage&q=chairs%20on%20the%20Titanic&f=false 23 May 2012.

Kouzes, J. M. & Posner, B. Z. (2003). The leadership challenge. NY: John Wiley & Sons, Inc.

Lamb, L. F. & McKee, K. B. (2004). Applied public relations: Cases in stakeholder management. Mahwah, New Jersey: Lawrence Erlbaum Associates.

Manske, F. A. (1990). Secrets of effective leadership: A practical guide to success. NY: Leadership Education and Development.

Martin, M. M. (1999, March). Trust leadership. Journal of Leadership & Organizational Studies. Vol. 5, No. 3, pp. 41-49.

Mayo Clinic. (n.d.). Exercise: 7 benefits of regular physical activity. Retrieved from http://www.mayoclinic.com/health/exercise/HQ01676/NSECTIONGROUP=2 May 21, 2012.

McGuire, C. U. III. (2007). The executive guide to the Baldrige Criteria: Improve revenue and create organizational excellence. Milwaukee, WI: American Society for Quality

McGuire, C. U. III. (2007). Definition of leadership. Personal communication in UMHB MBA Class.

McGuire, M. (1960). Communication back porch Paris, Texas. AKA Mom.

Northouse, P. (2007). *Leadership theory and practice.* Thousand Oaks, CA: Sage Publications.

Office Ethics Columns. (n.d.). The new loyalty: What bosses can expect (and what they can't). Retrieved from http://www.office-ethics.com/columns/loyalty.html dated Sep 5, 2012.

Pohl, M. (2000). Learning to think, thinking to learn: Models and strategies to develop a classroom culture of thinking. NY: David McKay Co. Inc.

Powell, C. L. with Persico, J. E. (2003).My American journey. NY: Random House.

Reynolds, S. (2012). Why people fail: The 16 obstacles to success and how you can overcome them. San Francisco, Jossey-Bass.

Senge, P. M. (1990; 2006). The fifth discipline: The art and practice of the learning organization. NY: Doubleday.

Spink, K. (1997). Mother Teresa: A complete authorized biography. NY: HarperCollins.

Thomas, K. (2008, Nov/Dec). The four intrinsic rewards that drive employee engagement. Ivey Business Journal. Retrieved from http://www.iveybusinessjournal.com/topics/the-workplace/

the-four-intrinsic-rewards-that-drive-employee-engagement  May 21, 2012.

U.S. Army. (1983). Military leadership (FM 22-100). Washington, DC: U.S. Government Printing Office.

United States Office of Personnel Management. (2001, 3 January). A handbook for measuring employee performance: Aligning employee performance plans with organizational goals. Retrieved from http://www.opm.gov/perform/wppdf/handbook.pdf  May 22, 2012, pp. 50-56.

United States Office of Personnel Management. (n.d.). Best practices: Mentoring. Retrieved from website http://www.opm.gov/hrd/lead/BestPractices-Mentoring.pdf  May 21, 2012.

Urban Dictionary. (2012) Seagull Boss Definition. Retrieved from http://www.urbandictionary.com/define.php?term=seagull%20boss not dated.

Visual Teaching Alliance. (n.d.). Visual impact, visual teaching. Retrieved from http://www.visualteachingalliance.com/ dated June 5, 2012.

Wilson, S. B. & Dobson, M. S. (2008) (2nd ed.). Goal setting: How to create an action plan and achieve your goals. pp. 4-9. NY: AMACOM.

Made in the
USA
Middletown, DE